The Smell of Incense, the Sound of Silence

by John W. Groff Jr.

Forward Movement Publications, Cincinnati, Ohio

©1988. Forward Movement Publications, 412 Sycamore Street, Cincinnati, Ohio 45202. Printed in U.S.A.

Merciful God:
 Take from us our eyes
  that we might see;
 Take from us our ears
  that we might hear.
Give us new hearts
 that we might know.
For the sake of the One who
 multiplied paradox upon paradox,
Even unto the ultimate paradox
Of showing us that only
 from death comes life;
For the sake of the One
 who came that we might
Become who we always have been.
Even Jesus Christ, your Son, our Lord.

                    Amen.

The Rev. John W. Groff Jr. is an Episcopal priest, poet and "itinerant" meditation teacher who lives in Guntersville, Alabama.

For Boots
Who shows me anew each day that it is all true.

The gratitude of the author is here expressed to the Rev. Caryl J. Altizer and Ms. Boots Groff who read the manuscript and offered many penetrating and helpful suggestions.

The calligraphic rendering of the prayer which opens this volume as well as the title pages introducing each chapter represent one of the gifts which God has given to Ms. Ginny Dixon. Any words of thanks I might offer her for her contribution to these pages would be inadequate in the extreme. Suffice it to say that I consider her one of God's special graces in my life.

Although one of my proofreaders repeatedly called my attention to the fact that I had failed to use the currently popular "inclusive language" in writing this book I have consciously chosen not to do so. Such syntax I find artificial and awkward.

Readers of both sexes will however readily discern from the text that not only do I ascribe completely to the theory of the androgynous nature of the human race but also that my experience of God is such that I cannot but believe that this is so of the Deity as well.

With the exception of the first poem, where the use of the double pronoun seemed effective, I have therefore used the masculine throughout. This use, while fully intentional, is, however, intended to be generic rather than specific.

Foreword

Some years ago I had the temerity to sit down and write a book. Even as I did so I heard again, ringing in my ears, the counsel of a priest at whose feet I had sat in my seminary years and who once cautioned, "Never write a book, for the church will always thereafter insist that you be bound to what you have written. The church will never allow you to grow beyond that point." This sage advice notwithstanding, *The Mystic Journey*[1] was ushered into print. Its final chapter was devoted to Thomas Merton, the twentieth-century priest, monk, poet, mystic who was then and remains today my *guru*, my spiritual teacher and master. An irony is that Merton's best known work remains, even after more than thirty-five years, his autobiographical *Seven Storey Mountain* which was written in his spiritual infancy and which in the later years of his life he categorized as being hopelessly parochial and which he stopped just short of disowning as far too narrow a view of the nature of the intercourse between God and the human soul, the God within. When I wrote *The Mystic Journey* I was aware of Merton's feelings about *Seven Storey Mountain* and I knew the cautions of my old theology professor. I wrote it anyway.

In the intervening five years I have said a hundred times and thought a thousand times that were I to write *The Mystic Journey* today, it would be a very different book. It would not be a primer, a basic introduction to Christian mystical experience, drawing on the thought and reflections of the church's thinkers in this, the ultimate area of life, so much as it would be a kind of statement of the thoughts and reflections and convictions of an individual who was consciously on the Journey, had reached a specific place on that Journey and who knew that tomorrow he would in all likelihood not be at quite that same place.

Growing tired no doubt of these oft-repeated words, my wife, my family, my friends, and those who have listened to my workshops, sermons, and conferences on mystical experience, have continued to encourage me to rewrite the book, or barring that, to write another one from a completely different perspective.

That perspective (and the reader is herewith forewarned) is experiential. What follows in these pages is decidedly *not* theology in the sense that we in the western church understand the meaning of that word. Parenthetically however it may be said that in the sense in which the ancient eastern church fathers spoke of the theologian as being "one who prays," it is in fact very much a book about theology.

Further, much of the content of this book will be found to be decidedly unorthodox. I sometimes even begin my lectures by saying (only half-jokingly) that if any of this were to reach the ears of my bishop my heresy trial would begin the following morning. (Still, the long arm of episcopally-defined orthodoxy has left me relatively free to be who I am, and my brother and sister priests go their own way with bemused indifference.) It is then a book which is not for everyone and comes equipped with a warning like the one on a package of cigarettes.

Finally and again, what I write is not speculative theory; rather, my words reflect as accurately as I can make them my own experience. I agree with Swami Abhishiktananda (Father Henri Le Saux, OSB) that "No one (should) speak of an experience except the man whose heart has been captured by that experience."[2] I write from the perspective of one who has experienced the trauma and agony of divorce; who has been bedazzled by the blinding light of the joy of the discovery of new love incarnated in another person and who has hence remarried; of one who has been blessed with the grace of being part of the spiritual fellowship of a contemplative religious order as well as with the grace of being simultaneously father-in-God to and fellow sojourner with the souls of two truly unique and very different parish churches; of one who has been entrusted with the unspeakable gift of the sacred priesthood; of one whose basic faith orientation—at least in this present incarnation—has always been and remains Christian; and of one who has consciously (at least for the past seventeen years) believed that there is an incalculable depth in God into which each of us is bidden enter but which few of us dare plumb.("Many are called...few chosen"?)

I have no need to be "right" nor to be doctrinally correct; my experience is that the former need, in the case of individuals or of nations, inevitably results in conflict, and the latter in the creation of martyrs. I have, rather, a need simply to be honest. What is contained herein are *my* convictions concerning the spiritual life, born of *my* experience of the Holy. They need not

2

be that of the reader. Nor need they be that of the body faithful. In a word, I have reached a point in my life and on my journey where my karma has run over my dogma.

So, while I am acutely aware of Lao Tzu's contention that those who know do not speak and those who speak do not know, I am nonetheless convinced that without the use of words we cannot hope to go beyond words.

Therefore let us begin...

JWG+, aoar
Feast of the BVM, 1984

Footnotes

1. Cincinnati, Forward Movement Publications, 1979.
2. Abhishiktananda (Fr. Henri LeSaux, OSB), "Christian Sanny-asis", in *The Clergy Monthly*, Supplement IV, Bangalore, 1958, p. 48.

MYSTICISM

Scripture and Contemplation, Sin and Spirituality

yes, the gong is struck
again
the gong that is no
gong
which utters no
sound
discernable to the outer ear
(least of all to the one who tolls)

the gong that heralds new
beginnings
but
nothing ever ended
or
began

for all is ever
the same
all is ever
happening
ever
perfect

even now
even then
(there is no now, no then)

there is only
the one
who was and
is and
is to
come
the Alpha/Omega
Omega/Alpha

and judymichaelsarajohn
johnsaramichaeljudy
is His/Her
name

because He/She dreams
them
and thus they
are
and ever shall
be

like
epiphany
and st mary's
above, beyond, transcending
time

only one
parish
one person
one life

enfolded forever in
the arms of
His/Her/Their
agape
love

and thankful

1

...But before we do that, there are some decisions I made in sitting down to write this book and, in fairness, you need to be aware of them.

First and most important, I want you to be aware that I am not going to *teach* you anything whatsoever. Absolutely nothing that I have to say to you will be new. Everything in these pages is known by you already. You see, God loves each of us so very much that in creating us he has implanted within us from at least the instant of our birth, and very possibly from the milisecond of our conception, all we need in order that we might attain to that state of divine oneness with him which is his perfect will for all of his creation and therefore our ultimate destiny. (And which, incidentally, is already a realized fact even though we aren't generally consciously aware of it—but that's getting ahead of ourselves.) You already know all I have to tell you. The only problem is that you don't know you know. The only thing missing is awareness. So understand from the outset that this is not a textbook; it will not teach you a thing.

Nor is my intention to *explain* anything to you. As a matter of fact I intend to avoid assiduously saying anything that might even slightly smack of explanation. I covenant with you here and now not to do that—honest! There is a very good reason for *this* too. To explain something is to wind up with explanations and it is not explanations which our hearts hunger for but something else. Or rather, some One else.

Kahlil Gibran, that magnificent Lebanese saint, so misunderstood (Most, if not all, saints are misunderstood so don't aspire to sanctity if you want to be well thought of by the brethren. Or, as an old Sufi story puts it, if your house is too small for an elephant, don't marry an elephant trainer.) says it this way:

The teacher who walks in the shadow of the temple, among his followers, gives not of his wisdom but rather of his faith and his lovingness. If he is truly wise he does not bid you enter the house of his wisdom, but rather leads you to the threshold of your own mind.[1]

My second decision was to write with an *evocative* voice. In other words, I write with the intent of evoking, of bringing forth from you, a response of "Ah-ha! That's what I've felt all along!" Or, as our English friends are fond of saying, a sense of the penny dropping.

There is one word of caution and then we really can begin. Normally when we read nonfiction we do so with a kind of "mental pen" in our hands (if not in fact a real one). And we use it to underline passages which the internal computer of our minds tells us are important.

Don't.

Don't use either.

Not the pen or the computer.

You see, what I am going to say may be so outrageous that it will either short-circuit your computer or instruct you to relegate the book to the limbo of all forgotten things before you get half way through the first chapter.

Instead, read this book with your "third eye"; listen to it with your "third ear."

You do *so* have one. Of each.

Your third eye is your "inner eye," your third ear your "inner ear," intuitive sense organs through which the "really real" or the Ultimate Reality enter. Those "ah-ha" experiences. Remember, for example, the first time you saw *her* (or *him*) across that crowded room? You didn't need to process a whole data bank of statistics (five feet, three and one-half inches tall, blonde hair, blue eyes— with just the right twinkle—thirty-six/twentyfour/thirty-six and a half, obviously intelligent...) you just *knew*. Or perhaps you can remember the first time you went to the altar to receive the sacrament and suddenly you knew this really *was* more than simply a way Christians spend an hour on Sunday morning. You knelt at your usual place at the rail, cupped your hands, looked up expectantly and—wham! zowie!—what the priest placed in your hands was no longer what Mother Church *said* was the body of your Lord Jesus Christ; it *really was* the body of your Lord Jesus Christ. You didn't know *how* you knew; you just *knew*. And it didn't matter to you how you knew. That's the kind of thing I mean. Don't read the book—let it *happen* to you.

Now remember, we have to use words in order to go beyond words— beyond words so we might attain to experience, to The

Experience beyond words. To the experience of God. In fact, as we will see, words make no sense until they cease to make sense. As Merton once said,

Words create history, But they, in turn,
Must be destroyed by the history they have created.
The word supersedes the event, as light emerges from darkness
Transforming the event into something it was not.
But the event, in turn, supersedes its interpretation as darkness
Replaces light, and in the end it is darkness that wins.
And the words of the historian are forgotten.[2]

In the end the words will all fall away from the pages and what will be left will be only yourself. And God. But there will not be two of you sitting there. There will be but One.

Now we really are ready to begin.

There is no such thing as mysticism.

Yes, I know this is a book about mysticism. But I'll say it again. There is no such thing as mysticism.

Let me tell you a story. Once upon a time; in a land far, far away, near the Great Monastery, there was a lake. In that lake there was a family of striped bass. There was a mommy striped bass, a daddy striped bass, and, in time, a baby striped bass. Now, sad to tell, the baby striped bass was not terribly smart. One day the baby striped bass swam over to his mother and said, "Mommy, what is this thing everybody talks about, this thing called water?" "Why you foolish baby striped bass," exclaimed the mother. "It's all around you!"

And so it is with mysticism.

There is no such thing as mysticism because *all* of life is mystical. As soon as we begin talking about the "mystical life" or "mysticism" we posit the existence of a door with a blinking red light and marked "mystical door." It's part of living a life with a hundred-hundred doors with blinking red lights and marked something else, something different.

8

We partition off our lives in the same way we partition off the rooms in our houses. Hence we live an illusion because each life is an entity, the whole of it a unity, a oneness.

How many parts are there to our lives? How many compartments? How many rooms? How many doors?

The three doors (they are one door).

1) The door of emptiness. Of no-where. Of no place for a self, which cannot be entered by a self. And therefore is of no use to someone who is going somewhere. Is it a door at all? The door of no-door.

2) The door without sign, without indicator, without information. Not particularized. Hence no one can say of it "This is it! This is *the door*." It is not recognizable as a door. It is not led up to by other things pointing to it: "We are not it, but that is it—the door." No signs saying "Exit." No use looking for indications. Any door with a sign on it, any door that proclaims itself to be a door, is not the door. But do not look for a sign saying "Not-door." Or even "No Exit."

3) The door without wish. The undesired. The unplanned door. The door never expected. Never wanted. Not desirable as door. Not a joke, not a trap door. Not select. Not exclusive. Not for a few. Not for many. Not *for.* Door without aim. Door without end. Does not respond to a key—so do not imagine you have a key. Do not have your hopes on possession of the key.

There is no use asking for it. Yet you must ask. Who? For what? When you have asked for a list of all the doors, this one is not on the list. When you have asked the numbers of all the doors, this one is without a number. Do not be deceived into thinking this door is merely hard to find and difficult to open. When sought it fades. Recedes. Diminishes. Is nothing. There is no threshold. No footing. It is not empty space. It is neither this world nor another. It is not based on anything, because it has no foundation, it is the end of sorrow. Nothing remains to be done. Therefore there is no threshold, no step, no advance, no recession, no entry, no nonentry. Such is the door that ends all doors; the unbuilt, the impossible, the undestroyed, through which all the fires go when they have "gone out."

Christ said, "I am the door." The nailed door. The cross; they nail the door shut with death. The resurrection: "You see, I am *not* a door." "Why do you look up to heaven?" *Attolite portas principes vestras** For what? The King of Glory. *Ego sum ostium*** I am the opening, the "showing," the revelation, the door of light, the Light itself. "I am the Light," and the light is in the world from the beginning. (It seemed to be darkness.)[3]

"...and the light is in the world from the beginning." And nothing else is. *Nothing* else is. Or was. Or ever shall be. Only that Light. Which is God's love for us. For *all* of us.

Be careful now. Take a deep breath before going any further. Yes, that's what I said, God loves *all* of us. His whole creation. That Light shines on the trees behind my house and on the barking dog that disturbed your sleep last Friday night, and on old, quarrelsome Mr. Jones in the next pew, and on Aunt Henrietta, and on the Russian bomber pilots, and on the...wait a minute!!

Oh yes, on everybody.

I said in my sermon on the Sunday of the Beirut massacre that God loved the militant Muslim who drove the explosive-laden truck into the sleeping Marines no less than he loved the baptized, Christian Marines themselves. Four people in the congregation fainted.

As much as we would like to compartmentalize the Light and its Source and make God exclusively ours it simply won't wash because the Russian bomber pilot and the Muslim militant and the ax murderer you saw on the late news last night all *are*. They all are. They're walking around. Breathing the same air you and I are. And the fact that they *are* means that they are known by God and so are in the Light, and loved. To be known by God *is* to be; to be unknown by God is not to be. Let's try it again, just to be sure we all have it. A simple equation will do:

In the Light/Known, i.e., loved by God=To *be*.
Not in the Light/Unknown by, i.e., not loved by God=*Not* to be. (Or, to be not. Or, to cease to be.)

---

*Attolite portas principes vestras: Latin, "Lift up your heads, O gates." (Ps. 24:9).
**Ego sum ostium: Latin, "I am the door." (John 10:7).

As one spiritual master has put it, "To be unknown by God is altogether too much privacy."[4]

Such a radical understanding of God's love is hard for us because it disallows us the easy categories into which we squeeze not only him but everyone else. Surely some must be on the inside. Surely some must be on the outside.

No.

There are only people. Without category. All of them are God's children, and all are loved and cherished by him, and all of them are mystics. All who *are* are mystics.

Mysticism, you see, is rooted in the love of God. Not our love for him but his love for us, a love which transcends any logical, rational, or objective system we might like to use to limit it. Mysticism is the heritage of all persons; the universality of contemplative experience, of contemplative spirituality. At this deepest level of interaction between Creator and created, between the Lover and loved, the experience of that Light, of that Love, is the same for Christians as it is for Sufis. It is the same for Hindus as it is for Buddhists.

We strain to understand anything so broad, so deep, so all-encompassing. Of course we don't understand. We are not invited to understand God's love, we are not invited to understand mysticism; we are invited to *know*. To know while knowing that in the deepest sense nothing can be known.

This, of course, is paradox. Paradox is the only way we can experience it. We intuit it but as soon as we try to explain it we fail.

So we are left with but one viable alternative. And that is simply to continue to *be*. To be who we are: the beloved of God. To be mystics.

For Christians the paradox is concretized in the person of Jesus, the Christ. The cross Jesus tells us to pick up and bear is our inability to contain him, while at the same time longing so desperately for him.

(This is probably a good time to repeat something. Don't try to grasp any of this, conceptualize it, make sense of it. Simply let it happen. Hang around awhile longer and allow the paradox to do its work in you. It will.)

For Christians the paradox is concretized in the person of Jesus. It is in the person of the mystical, cosmic, Christ that we who are baptized find our destiny. We are people of that unspeakable union of love which the church calls the Holy Trinity. We are *not* the people of the book, of the Bible. For us the Bible has but one purpose and that is to tell us a story. And there is only one story and but two figures. The story is how it is that God realizes mystical union with us. The two figures that fill every page are God and the reader. *I* am the leper whom Jesus heals, the thief pleading for mercy on the cross, the other thief, taunting; *I* am Judas. And Peter. And Matthew. And all the rest. *I* am the nation of Israel, led out of slavery to freedom.

The story reaches its zenith not, surprisingly, in the gospels but rather in an obscure prophet named Hosea. For it is here that the unconditional love of God for me, for you—for the reader— takes on a concrete character with which I can identify. (The cross I can never hope to, nor am I supposed to, identify with; that act is and ever shall remain beyond my comprehension.)

Hosea is one born to privilege. He lives in a mansion with servants on every floor, has a VCR for every TV and a TV in every room. Hosea has a sunken bathtub, eats nothing but lobster tails and *filet mignon*, the former served with drawn butter, the latter marinated for at least twenty-four hours in straight Kentucky bourbon and soy sauce and then charbroiled medium rare. Hosea drinks nothing but Chateau Mouton-Rothschild, vintage 1924. As a matter of fact, he gargles the stuff. Hosea has need of absolutely nothing.

Then Hosea falls in love. With a whore.

Let's be absolutely certain that we understand this. Gomer is not a prostitute. Nor a lady of ill repute. Nor a member of the world's oldest profession.

Gomer is a whore.

Hosea falls madly, passionately, in love, and he marries her. They live happily ever after. For awhile.

Until one morning when Hosea wakes up to find his beloved gone. What does the lover do? What would you expect a lover to do? He goes out looking for her. He devotes the rest of his life to looking for her. He travels all over the county looking for her. And then the state. And the next state. And the next. Looking for his beloved, the whore.

When he runs out of pocket change to continue the search, he writes a check. And another, and another. When he overdraws his checking account he draws on his passbook savings. He cashes in certificates of deposit, and the AT&T stock. When that is gone he sells the cars and the house and the condominium in Key West. He never stops looking.

One day he finds her. On the auction block in a town square of a place far, far away. No longer is she young and beautiful. No longer do her breasts push against the confines of the material of her blouse. No longer does she toss her head disdainfully at the stares of men. Gomer is old and wrinkled and grey. Her hair hangs in dirty strands across her lowered face.

What does Hosea do then? Yes, of course he does. He spends his last red cent to buy her back. And then he takes her home with him.

Incredible? Certainly. But love does such things.

Who is the story about? God and the reader. God and you; God and me. Hosea is God. I am Gomer. You are Gomer too.

What is the story about? The story is about that mystical love which defies explanation, that mystical love between the Creator and the created. It is about the only thing that really *is*, the only thing in the world.

What is the Bible? The Bible is a love story which begins with a divorce.

Why have we been given the Bible? For the same reason that the *maitre de* in a restaurant hands us a menu when he seats us. In order to tell us what is available. We aren't supposed to eat the menu; it points to what lies beyond itself; to that which we hunger for. When he have ordered we give it back.

Just so.

The Bible is not our Mystic Lover. The Bible is not the one who calls us into mystical union with himself. It is a book which proclaims that such a One is and that he, Hosea to our Gomer, will sell all to find us and to consumate with us that love which has been since before the world began.

Hosea's story ends with Gomer going home. Did she eventually run away again to ply her trade? Or was she faithful this time? We're not told.

One thing is certain however. (This is important for us because our life with God—the mystic life—is analogous to Gomer and

Hosea.) If Gomer remained with her lover she must have in some way *responded* to his love for her. This is the true meaning of a word we hear bandied around so much in church. The word is *faith.*

Faith is the reciprocity of Divine Love. It has nothing to do with belief (There! Aren't you relieved after all these years?) In fact it is not cognitive at all. The person of faith is the one who falls into, with loving abandon, what most of us spend a lifetime running away from. *While not having the slightest idea what the consequences will be.*

The incarnation of faith we call *prayer.* Or, stated differently, prayer is our loving God. Prayer is a bonding of the heart to God. Or, to be really honest, I don't know what prayer is. Only God can teach us to pray and it is only he who can define it. (No! No! The church does *not* either teach us to pray. The church teaches us how to *say* prayers. There is a difference.)

So I can't help you with a definition here, but I think that's okay because I have a deep intuition that to define prayer is to miss the point and the point which you miss is the definition.

It's like trying to see your own eye seeing.

It's the answer asking the question.

And so we return to paradox. The incarnation of our response to God, of our faith, is something we call prayer and we do not even know what that means. This leaves us frustrated. We have been taught since childhood that every question has an answer and that we must understand.

Let me give you an image. It won't help you to understand but it might "lead you to the threshold of your own deep knowing." Then you won't need to understand.

A woman has lost her child. Only a moment ago, or so it seemed, her daughter had been playing contentedly in the back yard while the mother was washing the breakfast dishes. Now she is gone. Toys lying on the grass next to the swing.

Behind the neatly trimmed suburban yard there is a large patch of woods and to them the mother is instinctively drawn. All but panic-stricken, she runs into the woods. The dishes are forgotten. Tonight's supper is forgotten. *Everything* is forgotten save only the task at hand—she must find her little girl.

She calls the child's name. Again. Over and over she calls the name. As she calls she runs deeper into the woods, her feet crashing through the fallen leaves, her skirt catching on the lower branches of the trees. Then she realizes something; even if her lost child were to cry out in response, she wouldn't be able to hear her because of all the noise she herself was making. She stops and listens. That listening is so absolute and so total and so intense that it is a singular act which involves every facet of her being. It is not her ears that are listening; *she*, the entire mother, is listening.

Before, the woods had seemed so silent, so still, but now the sound is so loud as to be deafening. The woodpecker at work becomes a jackhammer. The sparrow's mating call is the screech of a fire siren. Every effort to be quiet has become another way of being noisy.

She sighs in quiet desperation for there is nothing left to do. And she knows it. She has tried everything and it has not worked. She becomes aware of that sudden emptiness deep within her heart which her little girl alone can fill. It is a deep chasm. Her eyes fill with tears.

At that very instant—at that instant when the mother *knows* that there is nothing more she can do—her daughter appears at her side, gently tugging on her apron. Two pairs of tear-filled eyes meet. The child, opens her mouth to speak. "Mommy?" she says, "I love you."

This is prayer. The sudden, unexpected manifestation of the presence of the beloved. The touching of that virginal point within you which belongs entirely to God and which is awakened only in those ecstatic moments of his manifested presence. This is real prayer, true prayer, absolute prayer. It is not *saying* prayers. It *is* prayer. And so too was every moment in the story which led up to that instant of the daughter's appearing—the looking, the crying out, and anguished searching.

The humble acceptance of your inability to surrender *is* your surrender. The humble acceptance that you do not know how to pray *is* your prayer.

This is what those who delight in labels and distinctions and categories call contemplative prayer, mystical prayer.

We are not here to categorize or to label. Like the searching mother who is not reflecting on the manner of her race into the woods (I really lost control. I wonder if I turned the hot water off before I left the kitchen), or on her torn skirt (It's a Dalton, my seamstress will never be able to mend it without those damned rips showing), or on the soreness in her throat caused by her impotent screams (I'd better go gargle right away), we need not classify degrees or states of prayer. We need simply to taste the moment that is, the moment of reunion with the object of our love.

That moment captures us completely. It gathers us into itself and, like the totality of the mother's silent listening, there is no space in the one praying for anything but the prayer. In fact the one who is praying in some sense actually becomes the prayer.

One of the first times this ever happened to me I was sitting on the ground in front of the meditation pool at the priory of my religious order in New Mexico. When I began my meditation the sky was clear and a gentle breeze—not even strong enough to disturb the surface of the pool—touched my face and hair.

I don't know how long I sat in the silent, ecstatic absorption of that Holy Presence (absence of need for watches is a grace of living in a monastery) but when that time of prayer had ended, I discovered that I and everything around me was covered with a quarter inch of snow!

This is the kind of absorption I am speaking of. It is total. It is complete. And it is very, very good. It is very, very right.

No, we can't define prayer. We can't say to one another, "It's this, and not that."* As a matter of fact we can't even make prayer happen. That is not our job. What *is* our job; what we *can* do; the *only* thing we can do, is create for and in ourselves an atmosphere in which prayer can happen. We can prepare ourselves for prayer, allow it to happen.

For you see, prayer is really very little about *doing* but very much about *being*. And of this we shall have more to say later. By using words. To go beyond words.

Almost twenty years have passed now since that December night on the island of Okinawa. That first night.

I had sat into the early hours of the morning—surrounded by filing cabinets, technical manuals, electronic equipment; all of the accouterments of modern technology—writing reports to be con-

---

*This is really because *all* of our life, everything in it, is prayer. But it's too early in the book for me to tell you that so forget I said it.

sumed, ultimately, by the great paper factory which the government of this country calls the Pentagon and which exists to plan and promulgate how God's children who have chanced to be born Americans can wage war against God's children who have chanced to be born other than Americans.

When I had at last finished, I sighed, leaned back in my chair, and lit a cigarette.

And it began.

That growing sense of peace. That dawning awareness of Presence. That experience of being suddenly no longer in that room but, instead, floating just beneath the surface of a great and infinitely gentle body of water which was gradually buoying me upward. Of being caressed by that water. Surrounded by it. Protected by it. Like the amniotic fluid in a second womb. And, again, that Presence. Permeating the water. In the room. With me. In me. Becoming me. And me it. And the knowledge, the intuitive knowledge, that I was safe and that all of this was all right.

That is the sum total of that night, of my first experience of the contemplative, of mystical awareness. Beyond these words I cannot go save to state categorically that I have never, never been the same. No one could possibly be.*

This prayer which we have spoken of as contemplation is not, just as the Bible is not, an end in itself. Rather it is a gift, a vehicle through which we attain an end—love—the reciprocal love of God which our tradition speaks of as divine union.

It is a gift not for a privileged few who are somehow "worthy." It is given to each of us. Yes, even you. (If you find this hard to swallow, wait until you see what comes *next*.)

Nor is the gift of contemplation given us at a particular moment in time, differing from every other moment in time; it is infinitely given in every breath and in every heartbeat. You have *always* had the gift. Which is the vehicle, the means to divine love, to union with God.

Yes, there are special moments, pivotal moments when, pierced by God's haunting beauty, you know you belong to him. But

---

*It would not be until many years later that I would discover that on that evening as I sat there unfolding within, awakening to myself, the Buddhist world was celebrating Wesak Eve, the night before Rohatsu, which is the anniversary of the enlightenment of Siddhartha Gautama, the Shakyamuni Buddha.

these are moments of knowing, moments of awareness, and *knowing* his Presence within is a very different thing from the objective *fact* of his Presence within.

For you see, our very origin is in contemplation. That is how we came to be: God contemplated us, each of us, in the depths of his own divine being, and we simply were. We simply came to be. And the very first thing he created in us was a perfect capacity for divine love, i.e., for himself. This capacity for himself, this *Capax Dei**, is man's state when we first encounter him in the opening two chapters of Genesis. An understanding of this will go a long way toward helping us understand the meaning of "sin" and "hell," of which we will speak a little later.

No one has said all of this better than the fifth-century saint, Augustine of Hippo, when he wrote that our hearts are restless until they find their rest in God.

Of course they are. Only the One who has created the emptiness can fill the emptiness.

So the gift of contemplation is eternally given; it is always there. And the only properly called "beginning" moment has nothing to do with being "saved" (there is in fact nothing to be saved from or for). Rather, it is that moment when the ache in my heart becomes so intense that I can no longer bear it. And in that moment, I cry out in my agony to the One I never knew and have always known.

It is the moment when the depth of the ache becomes the depth of the knowing, the moment when I know that I am in the Presence of God. It is the moment of *satori*. At this instant, although certainly I cannot articulate it, I intuit, with the Angelic Doctor, that

> The final attainment of man's knowledge of God consists in knowing that we do not know him, insofar that we realize that he transcends everything that we understand concerning

---

*Forgive me the Latin, it is so beautiful I couldn't resist it.

him.... Having arrived at the term of our knowledge we *know* God as *unknown*.[5]

That intuition is enough. That is all there is and all there need be.

Let me say it once more, for it is terribly important. These holy moments are beginnings only in the sense that they are the beginning of our *awareness* of God's love for us. They are *not* the beginnings of that love itself. That love has always been. Never, never has there been a fraction of a second when we were not living in that love. What we lacked was the awareness of his Presence.

The moment of awareness is the moment in recorded time which holds, within itself, every other moment of recorded time. It is a moment which transcends recorded and recordable time, a moment which is forever happening. It is a clock which is no clock and which is forever tolling, "I am now, I am *this* instant, I am that, I am."

For me that early morning in the room on the island is and ever shall be my dawn, my present, my eternal now. It is in such moments—and I use the plural intentionally; there may well be more than one—that we awake to what is and in that awakening forever fall asleep to that which is not. That which is not is not infrequently all the things we had held to be of supreme importance and ultimate significance.

A traditional metaphor is "journey." We say "Wow! That's a really holy person. He's come a long way on the 'Spiritual Journey'!"

There are two things wrong with this. First, it tells us how important to the church (and hence, presumably, to God), something called "spirituality" is. Mark well: God couldn't care less about your "spirituality"! What God cares about is *you*. Who God loves is *you*. Your "spirituality" and your achievements are of less importance to him than are the number of duckbilled platypuses (platypusi?) that fell from the sky yesterday.

I know this is hard to grasp, especially in a country weaned on a work ethic of gigantic proportions. In the United States of America our all-time favorite story teller—certainly in terms of

19

our having adopted lock, stock, and fishing pole his philosophy—isn't Mark Twain or Ernest Hemingway, but Horatio Alger. Most clergy don't help. Listen to the sermon next Sunday and count the exhortations to "do." "Lettuce"* theology is far removed from what we are concerned about here.

So again, God loves Father John. He doesn't have much of an opinion one way or the other about Father John's spirituality.

That's the first thing that's wrong with the spiritual journey metaphor. The second thing is the idea of "journey." It is a time-honored term and I used it in the title for my other book. What we are speaking of is not a journey at all. If we are going to be bound to that term then we must use it with the full realization that it is a journey from a place we have never been to a place we have never left. And a journey *within*. And a journey where the self who begins is not the self who arrives but the self who arrives is the real self who began because the *real* self was born having completed the journey before he started it.

I'm going to suggest a better metaphor. (As you probably have surmised, in this book we have all new answers to all the old questions. But that's why you bought it, isn't it?) The metaphor I want to use is that of "awakening" (which is what the Zen term *satori* which I used a page or two back and did not footnote means). Awakening as a metaphor for mystical experience, for mystical reality, is not my own term. It comes from Zen Buddhist literature. Should that trouble you, remember that all truth, no matter who speaks it, is of the Holy Spirit. So, it's to be awakening. Let me try to show why. Let's do a guided meditation together.

You are at Eucharist. It is one of those perfect celebrations. The celebrant is wearing your favorite chasuble; the choir has sung your favorite hymns; the acolytes have been like well-trained scrub nurses in an operating room, knowing what the priest wanted next before he had to ask for it; tranquility reigns.

Or . . . Your work is done for the afternoon and you have three whole hours before you have to do anything else. You walk leisurely down to the city park and stretch out under your favorite tree. For once there is no sound of traffic to disturb your silence. A fluffy white cloud slowly drifts by overhead.

*"Let us . . ."

Or... You're in your parish church. The sermon hymn is ending (thanks be to God—you only had to sing the first three verses this morning, not the whole thing), the curate enters the pulpit and begins his sermon (understand now—this is one of those sermons; not the usual fare).

And unexpectedly you sense God uniting you to himself in contemplative prayer. It is not a conscious decision on your part. It just happens. The feeling grows. It wells up within you. More and more and more intense. Until you feel as if you are absolutely going to burst! Or that you are going to shout with pure delight.

That's it!

These tastes of love create in us a need. Nothing satisfies that need. It is unfulfilled love, and once touched by it we are drawn to silent waiting in the solitude of our own aloneness.

We begin to seek opportunities to open ourselves to the possibility of such moments again and again and again; we *awaken* to the reality of the ecstatic love which God pours over and into us and awaken to our own capacity to receive and to reciprocate that Love.

We no longer resist. We surrender to the love of God. In the same sense that the Bible uses the phrase "to know," as in David *knew* Bathsheba." We give ourselves to be known to God. We give ourselves to the divine love and to the One who is its Source, and in contemplation we do that willingly, adoringly, with complete abandon. He *knows* us; he possesses us as a lover possesses the beloved. All duality, all "two-ness" ceases as the two become one flesh and one spirit. They are fulfilled, wholly one.

The one who sits is the one who knows.

I want to make it quite clear that the whole essence of contemplative prayer is that the division between subject and object disappears. You do not look at God as an object and you don't look at yourself as an object. You don't stand back and look at yourself, you are just not interested in yourself.[6]

Like the flower, suffused with the sun, we have *done* nothing but simply to sit there. In our sitting, in our *being* there, we have found our petals opening and we have delighted. We have become. We have awakened *to what we always have been.*

It is not that the flower was a toadstool before the sun kissed it. The flower was always a flower, it just was not awake; not fully opened to, and in the glory of, its flowerhood.

It is natural for a flower to be a flower. A flower cannot be anything but a flower. It is natural for you and me to be mystics. The only thing we can be are mystics. The only thing missing is our awareness of this. And the way we become aware of our mysticism is to awaken to what always has been, what always will be.

Let's take a break.

I find myself, like St. Paul, doing the very thing that I should not do. I find myself attempting to *teach* you things you already know because they are truths which lie within each of us, things which are ultimately unteachable.

If you find yourself at this point with a slightly boggled mind then take heart; you are exactly where you are supposed to be. I have *intended* to boggle your mind. In attempting to speak of mysticism we must transcend logic because logic is a creation of man's ego which attempts to control and systematize truth. It is an exercise in futility and the ultimate example of our foolhardy pride because we are seeking to capture and control what we ourselves are—truth itself.

Attempting to be logical about this, attempting to explain any of it is like...

•Being in a burning library, scanning the stacks for a dictionary so you can look up the definition of "fire."

•Or like the caterpillar who wakes up one day to the realization that today is the day he is going to metamorphize into a butterfly. He sets out to record the grand event. He checks his camera to make sure it is fully loaded and that the lens cover is off. He gets it set just right on the tripod. He adjusts the light meter and sets it on the automatic feed. He loads his cassette tape recorder and his VCR with brand new tapes and he sharpens his pencils and opens a fresh notebook. Now he is ready. And the metamorphosis begins. And the first thing to die is his brain! A butterfly, you see, is not a caterpillar with wings; a butterfly is a butterfly. So much for observing ourselves.

•Or it is like the man who lost his donkey and searched all over the world for it for years. One day he looked down and found himself riding on—his donkey, of course. You already "have" all this.

•Or it is like the chicken lying on her back with her feet up in the air. "What are you doing?" asks the rooster. "Holding up the sky," says the chicken. We're trying to find the God who has found us. We're trying to *do* when it is not about doing at all but about *being*.

•Or it's like the yogi who sat staring at his navel and fell in.

•Or like trying to eat your own mouth.

•Or it's like the novice Zen monk who sat for months at the gate to the monastery, hoping to be accepted as a student by the abbot. At last he was allowed to enter and when the meditation bell sounded for the first time he rushed into the *zendo* and sat down at the feet of the master and began to meditate. After about twenty minutes of this he suddenly looked up and asked the abbot, "What happens next?" "Nothing happens next," replied the master. "This is it."

•Or it's like the other Zen monk who went to the abbot perplexed and asked how long it would take him to awaken. "Ten years," said the abbot. So the monk meditated for ten years and nothing happened. He went back to the abbot and asked how long it would take him to awaken. "Ten months," said the abbot. Ten months of meditation passed and nothing happened. He returned to the abbot with his question. "Ten days," he was told. Nothing. One final time he asked. The abbot turned to his assistant, the head meditating monk, and said, "If he doesn't awaken in ten minutes, stab him with this dagger." And so he did. Awaken, that is.

•Or it is like the man who got up one Monday morning and found himself in the very depths of depression. He realized how much he hated his job, how dissatisfied he was with his wife, with his children, with everything in his life. Looking out of his bedroom window, his eyes chanced to fall on a beautiful, marvelous scene. Far, far in the distance, across a seemingly unnavigable body of water, was a magnificent island. On the island, an unscalable mountain. On the peak of that mountain: paradise. So what does the man do? Naturally he leaves everything behind, somehow swims the body of water (which is infested with man-eating sharks), climbs the mountain (during which he must do battle with an army of malevolent dwarfs), and at last he finds paradise. He rejoices. And he sings. And he dances. Then he pirouettes around the top of the mountain and discovers that he is...back in his own living room.

•You have always had it. It was always there. To try to become a contemplative, a mystic, is an exercise in futility. You have always been that. You were born that. That is who you are. The only thing missing was awareness. Awakening. To what is. It is only by renouncing your dependency on thinking that you awaken to this truth. And this renunciation is like your death because your concepts of God and of yourself are rooted in your conceptual thinking. God is not our concepts of him. He is infinitely more. We are not our concepts of ourselves. We are infinitely more.

Who then is God? If we cannot conceptualize God, can we speak of him at all?

The answer to the second question is, of course, "no." To attempt to speak of God, is futility born of pride. God is to be experienced, to be adored; we cannot "define" the One who defines us. Islam, and especially its mystical strain, Sufism, has always known this. Judaism once did. Christianity never has. But be of good cheer; God is not boggled by our idiocy.

We cannot capture God in our minds, in our understanding, any more than we can catch the wind in our hands.

For God is nothing.

Take a minute or so to collect yourself.

It has to be said like that. To do otherwise, to say God is "this" or "that" is to place limits. Things are limited. A pen cannot be a coffee cup. A chair can't be a desk. A running brook can't be a forest. God is *in* all of these things (or they, like us, would not *"be"*) but he is *not* those things himself. God is in *all* things but he is not the things he is in. God is no-thing—nothing. (Do you see the problem of talking about him now? Do you see where words lead?)

Perhaps we can quit speaking of the Unspeakable, give thanks to and for the blessed no-thing-ness of God, and go on to that

24

of which we can speak. Ourselves. (I'm not *sure* we can do that, but we'll try.)

Who are we?* We who are more than our concepts of ourselves. If we are all contemplatives, all mystics, what does that mean?

The mystic is the one who knows.

It is not given for us to speak of God, to conceptualize God. But what is given is infinitely more—to *know* God even as he knows himself.

And it is possible in this present life!

For you. And for me. It is, in fact, the norm for all mankind to do so. When it doesn't happen in this lifetime it may be because we have tried to make it happen.

In our pride we live out most, or all, of our lives like the people of Israel in the Old Testament, attempting to earn what we had all the time.

All we really had to do was not to *do* anything but simply *be* who we are and always have been in God's eternal love.

So the contemplative, the mystic, the awakened one, does not *do*. He simply *is*. There is nothing left to do. It has all already been done.

The contemplative is not the storied spiritual giant who goes about teaching others to pray. He does not know how to pray himself, but knows that God will pray in him.

The contemplative's prayer—if it is a prayer—is to offer the least resistance to the advances of God's love, understanding not at the level of answers but at the level of awareness.

The contemplative realizes that at every moment all that he has is literally out of his hands, that it is all an unseen giftedness.

The contemplative, in his awakening, has come to know that to pray is to do what water, ducks, clouds, and trees do. Prayer is simply to be yourself.

The contemplative is not a very religious person at all. The contemplative simply *is*.

Finally a few words (because that's all the subject deserves) about sin and hell.

*I promise to spend an entire chapter on this subject later in the book. Don't worry if what follows doesn't open doors for you. This is only a beginning.

25

Sad to say, if we look closely at a large part of what passes today for the body of Christ, the church, we discover the overriding emphasis not on an empty tomb but on a bloody piece of wood.

Listen (if you dare) to what issues from most pulpits on Sunday morning and from almost all those uniquely twentieth-century figures spawned by technological "progress"—the television evangelists—and you will hear the promise of retribution, wrath, and damnation. Fear, not joy, and certainly not peace, is the commodity sold fifty-two times each year to a listening people who can't get their wallets out fast enough to pay for this week's supply.

We believe more in our sins than we do in the love of God.

What is sin? I'll tell you what sin is. And here I *will* be didactic. This *is* a definition you can type on a three-by-five card and refer to each time you find yourself listening to a pulpit being pounded by a bellowing, salivating preacher.

SIN is being concerned about sin when we have the unconditional love of the Father.

You see, sin is not rooted in the love of God, and that which is rooted in the love of God truly *is*. Our sins do not matter; only the love of God matters. The cross and the empty tomb were the death of everything less than love.

Now, as for sin's bed partner, for hell.

Hell has two compartments, two chambers. Therefore, our final, irrevocable, last-word-on-the-subject definition of hell has two parts.

Compartment One
HELL is to realize for all of eternity what might have been. It is to realize forever what you have said "no" to all the times you said "no" to love.
Compartment Two
HELL is being eternally trapped in the inability to forgive yourself.

I refuse to end this chapter on such a note, so I will give you one more definition.

THE KINGDOM OF GOD is the unity of divine love. It is not a place, it is a moment.

And it has already come.

Footnotes

1. Kahlil Gibran, *The Prophet*, New York, Knopf, 1970, p. 62.
2. Thomas Merton, *The Strange Islands*, Trappist, Abbey of Gethsemani, 1952, p. 56.
3. Merton, *The Asian Journal*, New York, New Directions, 1975, pp 153-55.
4. Merton, *New Seeds of Contemplation*, New York, New Directions, 1972, p. 34.
5. Thomas Aquinas, *De Potentia in Boetium de Trinitate*, quoted in Merton, *The Ascent to Truth*, New York, Harcourt, 1951, pp. 100-01.
6. Merton, "The Life That Unifies", *Sisters Today*, Naomi Burton Stone, editor, 42:65, 1970.

MYSTICISM
in Daily Life

The rain falls.
The sun shines.
Seek to stop nothing which is.
Seek not to understand; for that is to grasp, to
possess, to own...and you are not the owner but
rather the one who is owned.
Let it be,
neither choosing nor judging
but accepting.

2

For every human being above the age of six months (an extremely arbitrary figure; my intuition is that it comes much earlier) there is at least one geographical, physical space where God "happens," a place where awakening occurs. It takes place within us, but we associate this happening with the place where we were physically when we became conscious of it. The Yaqui Indians and some of the Zen folks speak of this as "the right environment" or "the right spot."

As we grow older the number of such holy places increases. For me, one such place is Okinawa. Another is a tree outside the library at the University of Notre Dame. Another is a point on a two-thousand-foot mountain in Tennessee. (That place and its association for me with divine love would require, and deserves, another whole book. It is a place where butterflies rest in the palm of your hand; where wine is uncorked in adoration and consumed in thanksgiving; where bread is broken in awe and eaten in ecstasy; and where fullness is born from emptiness. Anyone, incidentally, who would question the reality of *creatio ex nihilo*, i.e., the creation of something from nothing, has never been in love.)

But the physical space I want to spend a little time talking about here is none of these....

Were you to be driving west on Interstate 40, toward Albuquerque, New Mexico, and were you to turn south on Highway 14 at Tijeras and follow that road to the town of Tajique, and then were you—by coincidence*—to turn right on the Fourth of July Canyon Road (just past the cemetery), and were you to drive oh, say, another five miles along that road (don't try it immediately after a snowstorm), you would find yourself at The Priory, at the Mother House of the Order of Agape and Reconciliation, seventy-two hundred feet above sea level, in the Manzano Mountains.

The order, sometimes called The Michaelites, is an ecumenical religious order for male and female contemplatives, founded by a priest of the Episcopal Church (he would tell you that to be more

---

*There is no such thing as a "coincidence."

correct one must say God founded the order) on the First Sunday in Lent, 1972.

Go ahead, drive through the gate and past the sign bearing the seal of the order and the legend, "Order of Agape and Reconciliation, Episcopal Sponsored, Semi-Monastic, Contemplative Community. No Hunting, Fishing, or Tree-Cutting; Contemplation, Meditation, and Prayer Only."

By the time you have driven fifty yards you will find that two of the largest dogs in the history of the world are trotting along effortlessly beside your car. (The sole exception to God's presence in *all* creation may well be the canine community. Especially in large canines who are part wolf.) These two are tame and gentle and somehow sensitive to those who, like myself, tend to perspire profusely when in the company of any dog too large to fit comfortably in one's lap.

Anyway, drive up the road, over St. Martin's bridge, pass the Shrine of Our Lady of the Manzano Mountains, and the three Trinity Houses where retreatants are lodged, and then park in the parking lot.

Take the brief walk up the path to The Enclosure (you'll see the heart-shaped contemplation pool on your right) and go on inside. Remember, now you are in silence. Holy silence. That silence is a grace; mercy within mercy within mercy. Take your time walking around. As the Father Founder once reminded me, there is no need to rush in a monastery. On the first floor you will discover several rooms: the refectory, the kitchen, a lounge, a cell named after St. Gregory of Nyssa, and one named after St. Macrina. That one was mine. On a wall on the first floor you will see a quotation from the *Talmud*. Don't read it now, we'll return to it later.

Take all the time you want. Look into the prior's office. And the prioress' too. Much of the surface work of the order is done in those two rooms. Not the *real* work, though. The real work is prayer. Prayer is done...well, let me tell you a story about that. To illustrate that.

One day a monk went to his abbot. "Father", he began, "May I smoke while I pray?" The abbot thundered, "Of course you may not smoke while you pray!" A few days later the same monk approached the abbot with a different question. "Father Abbot, may I pray while I smoke?" "Of course, my son. You may pray

anytime." And anywhere. And everywhere.
See what I mean?

Let's go upstairs now.

On the second floor you will find a well-stocked library, more guest cells, another kitchen, and the prior and prioress' apartment. Come back to this floor, especially the library, later. Right now I'm anxious for you to see what is on the third floor, St. Mary's Oratory, the chapel of The Priory.

Let the oratory happen to you. Just stand there for a time and absorb it, drink it all in. The icons. The carvings and the paintings. The hand-carved *Christus Rex*. The free-standing altar and the tabernacle containing the Blessed Sacrament.

Almost everything in this room has been made locally, by hand. (Few abominations to the Lord approach mass-produced sacred vessels and holy art. Those made by hand come into being filled with the prayer and the devotion of the craftsman; they are, in the true sense of the word, sacraments. Those from an assembly line are embued with an aura, with the stench of the profit motive. The difference is tangible.)

Stay here for awhile. Be still. Meditate. Perhaps light a votive candle. I'll come back for you later.

You're rested now from your drive? Good. I have something else to show you. Now that we've seen exquisite examples of man's handiwork, I want you to see some of God's unmediated handiwork.

Let's go outside.

Stop at the contemplation pool? Yes, I know. That pool is like a holy magnet to me too. It is as if it were the bearer of some great gift. Look closely (by not looking) at the statue of the Holy Mother. It's as though she were standing benevolent guard, arms extended downward in blessing. You'll recall my "snow meditation" here. Such quiet and peace at this place. As if the pool contains within itself all the water of the earth. If you sit here in meditation long enough you will come to feel as though you are drawn into its waters and are swimming lazily just beneath its surface. Calm. Peace. Utter stillness. Lady Julian was right: all will be well, all manner of things will be well. Her *anima*, the Virgin's *anima*, my own *anima*...all three reaching out and coalescing in a trinity of silent assurance that the feminine principle of receptivity and peace-giving love has made this moment her own, captured it in fond embrace. I surrender myself willingly and gladly to it.

We'll walk along the western side of The Priory, along St. Francis' Trail. We'll pass by St. Bruno's Hermitage which, incidentally, became one day the catalyst for my decision to leave this holy place (but not the order) and to go back into the world to live out my contemplative vocation.

We will go to Agape Meadow and its plateau and from there we'll look out over Mary's Woods and St. Bruno's Meadow. Then we will walk through St. Francis' Field and you will see the great Ponderosa Pines whose bark smells like vanilla ice cream. And the lava encrusted rocks telling a history of volcanos. Perhaps we will find there one of my very favorite natural icons, a nearly perfect fossil of a tiny fish imprinted on a boulder, seventy-two hundred feet above sea level!

Together we will behold the grandeur of this place. Perhaps we will somewhere simply stop, and sit for a time, and be, and know.

All of this we will do now in total stillness, in silence.

Yes, it *was* good, wasn't it?

You have what? Questions?

All right. I thought you might. Let's make a pot of coffee, get comfortable, and then we'll talk. What is it you would like to know?

Why did I ever leave? Do you remember the quotation from the *Talmud?* That's why I left.

> God did not create woman from man's head, that he should command her; not from his feet, that she should be his slave; but rather from his side, that she should be near his heart.[1]

That's why I left. I was in love with a woman whom I knew finally to be not another person, separate from myself, but rather to be the completion of myself. I have always believed that one of the reasons God led me to The Priory was to help me to understand that.

One day when I was in solitude, in retreat, at St. Bruno's hermitage, God wrote a poem in my heart:

Where was the
Glorified Christ
between
The Appearances?
Where is my
Love
for you when
You don't see
Me?
Always present

It was then that I knew I had to leave, then that I knew the purpose of my coming here had been accomplished.

Of such love I promise to say more later. For the present though, let me relate an ancient Sufi tale for you. It is attributed, not surprisingly, to Rumi.

One went to the Beloved's door and
    knocked.
A voice asked, "Who is there?"
He answered, "I am."
The voice said, "There is no room for you
    and me."
The door was shut.
After a year of lonely deprivation he
    returned and knocked.
A voice from within asked, "Who is there?"
The man said, "You are."
The door was opened for him.[2]

The coffee is good, isn't it? Here, have a second cup. Don't worry about the time, we have enough time. As a matter of fact, we have forever.

But you had more than one question.

Yes, that one I anticipated...

And you're right. *Anyone* can sit, can meditate, in a place such as this. *Anyone* can be a contemplative in such a place as The

33

Priory. But how do we live out a contemplative life in the world?. How can one be a mystic in the marketplace?

That question is what this chapter is about.

Environment is important, but it is far less important than we imagine.

The call to contemplation is universal. God has called all his creatures to realize their essential unity with him by participating in the depths of this experience. But the call to contemplation is not necessarily a call to the cloister. Generally it is not.

Let me tell you a story.

Just before my wife and I left for our vacation this summer, I received a long, painful, distressed letter from an old friend in another part of the diocese. My friend, whom I'll call Betty, poured out a tale of spiritual crisis which had led her to the point of despair over her home parish, the church in general, and her own place in God's mercy. Betty, a person who has been for as long as I have known her a serious and devout Christian, had found herself in what one sixteenth-century spiritual master termed, "the dark night of the soul." (It is ironic that only those who are really serious about their life in God have this experience. Most of us, content to spend a lifetime walking on the periphery of the Christian dispensation, never know it exists.)

Betty, a most articulate person, concluded her letter by writing, "Sometimes when I pray I feel so at peace, so filled, but when I have to face the world again with bills and disappointments and job worries it seems that the spiritual world and the 'real' world are so far apart—too far apart." Here my friend pinpoints the root of her discontent, without realizing what she has done.

Betty's world view is one-hundred and eighty degrees off reality, a perception she shares with the vast majority of mankind. It is not that which is without that is the "real" world; the "real" world—that which truly IS—is within. It is only in becoming fully at home in the interior and knowing that place as the one in which we truly live, move, and have our being, that we at last come to terms with and learn how to relate to that which is transitory, to that which is without.

Betty and you and I live in an age of incredible technological progress. We transplant human kidneys and hearts. It is yesterday's news to put a man on the moon. Lawmakers debate whether or not high school students should be required to demonstrate proficiency in computer skills to graduate. Mankind is fully capable of destroying itself in less than thirty seconds.

Like Esau and the Prodigal Son, we have sold our birthright for porridge and squandered our inheritance as ones who have been made in the image of God. For to be seduced by technology's siren song of ultimate value and the ultimate reality of what is outward and visible and tangible is to be bedded by a whore who will disappear, leaving us in dismay over what once seemed so concrete, so—well—real.

The ultimate journey (there's that second-best metaphor again) is a journey into interior, not outer space. It is a journey into ourselves and thus into God, for it is within ourselves, not somewhere "up in heaven" or "out there," that he dwells. It is a mystic journey, traveled by silent and imageless meditation, by allowing there to be spaces between the notes of our music, by smelling the roses and watching the leaves fall and hearing the water flow and by eating and drinking and making love. It is a journey into Ultimate Truth, into Pure Reality, into the One Who Is, into our destiny. The exterior environment in which we make the journey is not so important.

The call to contemplation is not necessarily a call to the cloister. *The call to contemplation is a call to be in the world in a certain kind of way.* For most of us it is a call to live in the chaos and the noise of the marketplace and by our presence there to transcend that noise, to bring silence and peace and thus to sanctify that chaos.

Radical? Of course. Radical to our ears because historically the church has taught us that there are two vocations. The first and the "holiest" is the vocation to the religious, the monastic, life. Those happy souls are to sit, to meditate, to pray, to be near God. These are the Marys, the contemplatives. For whom do they pray? For the rest of us, for the actives, for the masses who are the Marthas. Because the church has said it, we have believed it. This is unfortunate. And sad. Because it is not true. It is not the way it is.

It is a construct that creates divisions between persons, classes of persons. There are no divisions, or classes. There is only oneness. All is unity.

Did you feel a twinge of envy for those fortunate few whose environment is The Enclosure of The Priory at Tajique? Did you fantasize about how idyllic it must be for those silent, ghostlike, hooded figures passing to and fro in the paradise of the cloister?

It isn't. They have problems too.

The truth is that were you suddenly to find yourself locked away safely in the nearest branch house of The Order of the Society of Strict Silence and Scrupulous Solitude with only your "holy" brothers and sisters to share that space with, you would have problems, you would have distractions.

Were you suddenly to find yourself marooned on a desert island with no car pool to worry about, no braces to pay for, no noisy neighbors who have just bought the world's loudest sound system, no unbearable boss to pacify, and no quarrelsome mate to deal with, you would still have problems. Why? Because *you* would be there.

And *you* are the problem. For you. I am the problem for me. You get in your way. You hinder your own awakening, your own becoming. I do the same thing myself. We will talk more about this later.

No, there are no classes of people within the economy of God's creation; some holy, some not; some contemplative, some active. There are only people and all are one and all are monks, and all are....

Yes, that's what I said: everyone, including you, is a monk.

I received a letter from a dear friend, a member of a religious order, soon after I left The Priory and returned to the parish ministry. In her letter, my friend lamented that I was no longer a monk, that I had returned to being simply a parish priest. How surprised she was when I wrote back and told her that, like herself, I had been a monk from the day I was born and would be one forever.

All of us are monks. The noun "monk" is an anglicization of the Greek word *monos*, which means "to be alone." That is what we are, each of us. We are alone. John Donne was wrong: we *are* islands.

However, we are islands in a common sea. Each of us is lost with Christ in God. This is our basic identity as persons. Our external environment makes no difference. It is simply a physical context within which we live out our basic and fundamental identity. As contemplatives. As mystics. There are no distinctions.

The contemplative in the townhouse with three young children and a forty-year mortgage, can say to the contemplative in the Trappist monastery,

This is life in Depth—the *guha**—where
alone with God I am:
This life in the Depth, where alone in God I am;
This life in the Depth, where alone from God I am;
This life in the Depth, where alone is He who is...[3]

And the contemplative in the Trappist monastery can reply to the contemplative in the townhouse with three young children and a forty-year mortgage, "You know what I do—just go on."

We live from within. That which is interior is our environment; our context for being. That which is exterior is artificial and arbitrary and, ultimately, illusory.

So the contemplative in the city takes his environment, takes the "real" world, with him wherever he may go.

Awakened to the reality that all things have been given to him, that he contains all things, he is able to move easily and comfortably through his day and through whatever exigencies that day may contain. He is like a mirror, reflecting that which he encounters and yet remaining unchanged, untroubled, unsoiled, unaffected. Because the God within him is the personification of peace, the contemplative is himself at peace, in the city no less than in the monastery.

The mystic in the marketplace seeks nothing save that which is, in any particular moment, given to him. He prefers no particular thing to any other thing. He seeks not pleasure at the exclusion of pain but rather accepts with equally open hands pain and pleasure alike. The awakened mystic simply moves among other men seeking nothing whatsoever, accepting all things as they are. He does not seek to change anything. He has no need to change anything. He knows he is not on earth to effect change but rather to sanctify, by his presence, what he finds here.

Part of his awakening is the awareness of the fact that his every step contains within it the very union with God that men seek. When he sits, sitting is the Christ. When he eats, eating is the Christ. When he sleeps, sleeping is the Christ.

The mystic in the marketplace simply *is*.

---

*Sanskrit, "Cave." Used here as in "the cave of the heart," i. e. the interior self.

Least of all does he seek "experiences" of God. Knowing that he has been created not for experiences of God but rather that he might contain God within his very self, he knows that his lack of experiences is itself a grace and he is content with that grace. He *is* the experience which others seek.

In the parish church the contemplative is very likely to be the last person you would expect to be "spiritual." None of the manmade, which is to say "churchy," rules which we normally use to measure one another's piety seem to apply to him. He questions what good it is to be always doing something *for* God if you are never *with* God.

He does not understand life in terms of his acts, in terms of what he *does*, at all. He understands life in terms of who he *is* in the presence of God.*

Nor does he spend time in reflection. I once heard a speaker tell a group of people gathered for a workshop on the subject of "spiritual living" that the last question she asked herself before she went to bed at night was, "Well, Barbara, how did you do with Jesus today?" At the time I thought asking that question each and every night was the most wonderful idea I had ever heard. It isn't.

Reflecting, trying to have the insight, is like trying to swallow the sky. The insight is that we *are* the insight. The insight is that there is nothing, not even an insight, to acquire, for there is no one to acquire it. There is no insight other than the self we always have been, yet did not recognize. One day we suddenly realize that we had it all along.

The contemplative in the city is the one who knows that everything that is given to us in time—prestige, wealth, title, even

---

*Traditionally, the Christian mystic is not withdrawn from humanity, but is active both within the Christian community and the world at large. *Being* issues in *doing*. The experience of God's peace does not lead to quiescence and self-absorbtion, but moves the mystic to fulfill the great commandments to love God and neighbor, as well as self, in a life of service. The mystic works to promote the kingdom of God. For more on this subject, read in Thomas Merton's *New Seeds of Contemplation* and Evelyn Underhill's *Practical Mysticism*.

—The editor

insights—will be lost in time. He is the one who knows that only that which is given to us before time has any value.

And the only thing given to us before time is God's love.

In religious terms, this is simply a matter of accepting life, and everything in life as a gift, and clinging to none of it... You give some of it to others...Yet one should be able to share things with others without bothering too much about how they like it...All life tends to grow like this, in mystery inscaped with paradox and contradiction, yet centered, in its very heart, on the divine mercy.[4]

I am writing this book in a sleepy, little one-industry Alabama town which has a population of just over five thousand people. Thirty-five miles northwest in Birmingham there is a cloverleaf where three interstate highways join, parallel, and overlap one another. It is now almost three o'clock in the afternoon. Do you know what is going to happen at that cloverleaf at thirty minutes after three?

Rush hour.

Hundreds upon hundreds upon hundreds of cars, all going in excess of the speed limit, entering those three six-lane "super" highways from the four cardinal points of the compass and more. Faster and faster. More and more cars. Until...inevitably... Wham!

Rush hour.

You know, there is no ontology to rush hour. God never said, "Let there be rush hour." The only reason there is a rush hour *out there* (on that cloverleaf) is because there is rush hour *in here* (inside all those people). And inside you. And me.

Where are you going? What are you going to do when you get there? What is so important that it has to be done rightnow-soquickly...that...you...can't...possibly...be...enjoying... the...doing...itself?

What do we do when we get home? You know what we do: we turn on the TV. Or the stereo. Or both. We can't bear the silence. We are afraid of it. (And this is just another way of saying that we can't stand our own company.) Silence is contemptuous of the lie in ourselves. That's why we fear it. We intuit the truth in the mystic's statement when he writes, "Everything

39

within us came out of the eternal silence and will return to it," and that terrifies us.

What did you have for lunch today? By suppertime most of us can't even remember. Why? Because we never just *eat* at mealtime; we never just *taste* our food. Instead of eating when we eat we transact "business"; we talk to another person. (And that generally means that there are two monologues going on at the same time since we generally don't listen either.) When we can't find another person to have lunch with we buy a newspaper to read with our meal. Then we not only don't eat but we don't read either. Because both require a presence. Which we don't give.

Rush hour.

If rush hour has no ontology in God then it is a contingent reality which exists only in our own egos. And therefore it isn't real. And if it isn't real then it is an illusion. And if it is an illusion that we are caught up in and which gives us our identity and our justification for living then we likewise are an illusion. Then, we are not.

Another image, a quite different one.

A woman sits on the back porch of her home. It is late afternoon, about the time of rush hour. A gentle breeze stirs across the yard and caresses her face. She clears her mind of all thoughts and then concentrates on that breeze and how it feels on her skin. She becomes completely attentive to the "now" moment, to what *is*. She is not mentally projecting herself into the next hour when her husband will come home from the office. She is not physically on the porch and mentally at the bar mixing him a drink. She is not considering the alternatives for the evening meal. She is totally present to the present. *All* of her, the totality of that woman, is on that porch.

Her eyes wander among the flowers growing in the garden at her feet, and she looks at them (*really* looking, not absentmindedly looking; *seeing* the flowers) and suddenly she sees *it*.

What she sees she knows to be God's gift to her in that moment. Her mind assures her that there will be other gifts in other moments yet to be, just as there have been other gifts in other moments which have been. She turns her attention to none of these. She lives, every fibre of her being lives, in this time, in this instant.

What she sees is a spider, the most incredibly beautiful spider that has ever been. The *only* spider God has ever made. And he made it for her to enjoy. And she knows that. And so enjoy it she does.

She becomes totally absorbed in that spider. She *contemplates* that spider. Its basic blackness. The intricate yellow design on its back. The crazy-quiltness of its web.

In that moment there are for the woman but two creatures in all the world, the spider and herself. Gradually, even that distinction blurs, and fades, and finally disappears, and there is no longer a distinction at all, no longer any duality. The spider and the woman become one.

At *that* moment, in the instant of her complete presence to it, the moment itself becomes a sacrament—the moment is the presence of God.

Another such image. Several years ago I spent some time in that unique Central American country, Costa Rica. (It is unique for several reasons, not the least of which is that it has no standing army.) One night I found myself in a pizzeria for supper. (Pizza too, under the right circumstances, can be a sacrament of God. Much depends however on the temperament of the cook and on the temperature of the accompanying wine.)

As soon as I was seated I became aware of a certain presence in that dining room. Now it was a presence with which I am acutely familiar and one which I welcomed, but it was a presence which one does not normally encounter in the midst of rushing waitresses balancing Italian pies and pitchers of beer on trays as they hurry back and forth in cadence to the shouted orders, a blaring jukebox, and unnumbered conversations all going on simultaneously.

After I had given my order and tasted my wine, I allowed my eyes to wander amongst my dinner companions, seeking the source of the presence. And finally I found it. At a table in the far corner.

Two people sat there. Staring into one another's eyes. Deeply. Each drinking from the unfathomable depths of the other. Their pizza sat, untouched, in the middle of the table.

Forty-five minutes later, when I rose to leave, they were still there. Still being together. Still totally present to each other. Each openly available to that single self each saw in the eyes of the other.

This is how we contemplate.

41

The presence in that room was the presence of love.

As far as I know they are still in that restaurant contemplating one another, the pizza untouched. One thing I do know: the restaurant could never again be the same. Now it was hallowed.

How do I become the mystic in the marketplace, the contemplative in the city? How do I escape rush hour?

I escape rush hour by becoming the Self (big "S") who I am by nature instead of the self (little "s") who I am not but who I have become by training and by programming.

You see, ever since our childhood each of us has been educated to "fit in." Fitting in means to be useful and productive members of society, to adapt to the particular needs of society—needs defined by society.

Those who fit in are rewarded by the acceptance of the society. Those who do not are branded eccentrics and cast out, symbolic though such casting out may be.

For those of us who live and move and have our being in the United States of America during the waning years of the twentieth century, these "needs" are unquestionable world technological supremacy. "We" must out-tech "them." (Remember, for the mystic there is no "them;" for the mystic there is no duality.)

The reasons given for this need are usually vague, but they are based on the premise that it's them or us.

In such a society, success, upward mobility, and the accumulation of things all become supremely important, to be sought after, grasped, and—once obtained—jealously guarded at all costs.

Success, upward mobility, and the accumulation of things are not very high on the priority list of the contemplative person. In fact, the contemplative doesn't have a list.

But since earliest childhood very nearly every authority figure in the contemplative's life has told him that these values are ultimate and that if he is going to "make something of himself" he had better embrace them.

He had better get the right degree from the right university.

He had better join the right fraternity and so make the right contacts. (They'll be vaulable later on.)

He had better marry the right girl (from a "good" family).

He had better be a member of the right clubs. (And the right church.)

He had better have his name on the letterhead of the right charities.

He had better be promoted on schedule.

He had better be a team player...

And so the corporate banker and the computer programmer and the designer of weapons systems come to be of inestimably greater value to society than do the poet laureate, the composer of classical music, and the builder of sand castles. Not to mention the contemplator of spiders.

Don't you believe for a minute that the institution of the church is exempt from this mentality. The clerical order, that grand, round-collared, caste system, which proclaims the One in whom there are no distinctions, boasts its own standards and units of measurements as to what constitutes success.

The saddest thing of all is that the banker and the programmer of computers and the weapons system designer and yes, the priest too, are also contemplatives. This is their true nature, though they may deny it by "fitting in."

In denying what he is, in favor of that which he is not, in choosing the lesser over the greater, in saying "no" to his True Self, man—and society as well, for society is man writ large—prefers the darkness instead of the light. And this choice is made at the great peril of all.

You live the contemplative life in the city simply by living the *natural* life in the city, by being who you were born being. You live simply and unselfconsciously.

The woman on the back porch, being with her gift, is not conscious of herself at all. She is not saying, "Here I am, staring at this dumb spider and wasting time again. I wonder if anyone is watching. I wonder if my hair is straight."

The lovers in the restaurant were not in the least aware that a bearded priest was watching them from across the room.

The mystic is the one who is aware that he is because he is completely unaware that he is.

The contemplative life is the natural life, the unselfaware life, the loving life, the life wherein I am being myself.

On the other hand, the success-oriented, success-obsessed, upwardly mobile young executive whose mechanical megalith races daily toward its appointment with all of the other upwardly mobile young executives' mechanical megaliths on the cloverleaf in order that each might get as quickly as possible to their mortgaged condominiums and gulp (without tasting) their double martinis before punching tonight's program into their home computers so that tomorrow they can impress their bosses and hence gain rapid promotion so that they might do more of the same faster...are conscious of nothing but themselves.

Nor does the awakened contemplative living "in the world" trade one set of experiences—secular—for another set of experiences— "sacred" or "mystical." He knows that as long as there is a "me" left to have a mystical experience, he can't have one at all.

> It becomes overwhelmingly important for us to become detached from our everyday conceptions of ourselves as potential candidates for special and unique experiences, or as subjects for realization, attainment, and fulfillment.[5]

He does not have to go looking for experiences of any kind. He is awake to the beauty with which God has surrounded him and he takes delight in it, in the everyday. It is enough to be with God at a sunset. He is deeply aware of the reality of the holiness of the ordinary.

While he may well be found on a given afternoon meditating in a pew in front of the reserved sacrament in his parish church, he is just as likely to seek out a lake or a meadow or a mountain as the outer, the external, environment for his sitting. Then a leaf drifting soundlessly with the tide becomes his reserved sacrament. A drop of rain, his holy water. For the contemplative all of life is a sacrament. For the contemplative there is no such thing as *unholy* water.

Do not look for him where large crowds have gathered to create noise and confusion. Do not look for him, for instance, at football games or at a cocktail party. When he is with others it is much more likely that he will be found in a small group which has come together not to kill an evening with meaningless babble but rather to create new life in a place in time by simply being together.

44

His life style is one in which the motto has been reversed—"don't just *do* something—sit there."

More at home in small, intimate gatherings than in large, impersonal ones, he is—when not simply alone with the Alone—even more likely to be at peace with but one other who is, like himself, aware that he is a solitary other.

My wife and I arise early enough in the morning to ensure that neither of us has to leap immediately out of bed and into the shower and off to the activities of the day.

While music plays softly in the room,* we share coffee and cigarettes (remember—your every step contains the union that you seek: drinking a cup of coffee is a sacred act, smoking a cigarette is a sacred act) and the nearness of each other. And of God. Very little conversation is exchanged. What *is* exchanged is a communication that transcends the need for conversation.

Eventually, as the sun brightens the yard outside our bedroom door, and the blue jays and cardinals come to feed there, the tape player is turned off, and the coffee cups put down, and the cigarettes extinguished. Together, we sit in silent meditation. With one another and with the One who is the Source of all that is.

Finally, a few words about junk. The junk in our lives is composed of such issues as how George Jr.'s college tuition is going to be paid this month, what we are going to do about the shingles that are coming off the roof, whether or not we can get another winter out of the old Volkswagen—those kinds of things.

These concerns are as real for the mystic in the marketplace as they are for everyone else. The difference is that the contemplative recognizes them for what they are, which is to say he sees them from a different perspective, through a different set of eyes. Through the third eye.

He knows that being a contemplative is not measured by the *time* he has available but rather by his *desire*; he knows that all of the junk in his life is the preparation for the next manifestation

---

*I will say more about music as a pre-meditation aid in the next chapter.

of God's mercy. He knows that the obstacles are not the obstacles, they are the way.

If there is not enough money this week there is not enough money this week. If he can do something to change that and if he considers it important enough to change, he changes it. If there is nothing he can do about it or if he does not consider the change to be worth the compromises he will have to make to effect that change, he does nothing. He simply lets it be.

The contemplative is the one who is acutely aware that, like everyone else, he lives in the diaspora of his own compromises. He chooses them, therefore, very, very carefully.

The contemplative is willing to live without answers. Like the German Poet, Rilke, he chooses not to spend his lifetime in an endless and obsessive search for answers but instead, he simply lives the questions.

The contemplative is the one who is willing to be content with nothing.

In the course of giving a conference to the novices at the Abbey of Gethsemani one day, Thomas Merton spoke of a recent visitor he had had at his hermitage, a Buddhist monk from Viet Nam named Tcich Nhat Hanh.

The two, Merton said, had spent much of the previous night talking together about the years of formation each had had in his respective religious community in preparation for taking life vows.

"How soon after you entered the monastery did your abbot begin instructing you in sitting meditation?" asked the American Trappist.

"After about five years," was the reply.

"Five years!" responded Merton. "What did you do before that?"

"We were taught how to close doors like a monk."

The contemplative in the city is the one who knows how to close doors. And to open them.

3

It is late afternoon. The shadows of evening are beginning to spread and the sun, like some great red ball, seems about to be cradled in the hand-like peaks of the mountains lying to the west of the city park.

The moving van, relieved of its load, has just pulled away and the new family on the block has disappeared into the neat, ranch style house on the corner.

Inside the house the family of four looks around wearily at the cardboard boxes stacked unevenly in practically every available foot of space. How long it will take to unpack. How much work lies ahead before this house becomes their home. As has happened innumerable times today already to each, the thoughts of the teenage girl move to the home and the town and the friends left hundreds of miles behind just two days before.

As the father closes the front door the mother moves to a box marked for easy identification, and the son, forgetting that it has yet to be turned on, reaches to take the phone off its hook.

First removing their shoes, they enter the smallest of the bedrooms together. The box is opened and from it are taken a crucifix, a box of incense sticks and an accompanying boat, a small throw rug, several oblong pillows, and a cassette tape player.

Each of these articles is placed strategically—the crucifix on the wall, a stick of incense in the boat, on the rug which has been laid in the center of the floor; the tape player in a corner; and pillows at irregular intervals around the room.

While the mother lights the incense the father selects a tape, places it in the player and turns it on. The room is filled with the gentle sounds of music, the soundtrack from the motion picture, *Chariots of Fire.** Not a word has been spoken.

The four members of the family arrange themselves comfortably on the pillows. The mother, who suffers from a chronic back problem, braces herself against a wall.

As the smell of the incense and the sound of the music gradually permeate the room, each person allows the thoughts and the

---

*An appendix providing some suggested music for pre-meditation begins on page 102.

49

concerns of the twelve-hour day just past to move first through, and then out of, his mind. Each focuses on the music, buoyed by it, floating with it. There are no more concerns. There is no more unloading to be done. There is nothing...but the music.

After a time, the father reaches across his body and pushes the button which turns off the tape. The room and those in it are immersed in silence.

Were we able here to enter into the being of these four persons at this point this is what we would observe. We'll begin with the daughter.

She is seated comfortably. What is comfortable for her, however, may be uncomfortable for her brother and her parents: the positions of the others vary. In her case she has crossed her legs in the "semi-lotus" position. Her back is straight; her head tilted slightly forward; and her hands, resting in her lap, are joined in such a way that the right rests in the palm of the left with the thumbs slightly touching. Her eyes are closed and she is breathing slowly and regularly through her nose.

As she breathes in she mentally repeats the word, "Jesus." As she exhales the word changes to "Mercy." "Jesus...mercy...Jesus...mercy." This is her mantra.

Were we able to enter into and observe her parents and her brother, we would note differences here as well. The mother coordinates with her breath the words "Abba" and "Father." The father, who first began to meditate while serving with the army in the orient, has always used the single word, "Mu."

Gradually, the girl's entire being settles gently into the silence which is at the core, at the center, of her being. Gradually, she becomes aware as she has become aware many times before, of her essential oneness with her Creator, with herself, with her family, with the room in which she sits, with all things. Were we to ask her later how she knew these things she would be unable to tell us. She is aware because she is unaware. She knows by unknowing.

As this begins to happen she allows her mantra to slip away and she becomes completely enveloped in the silence of God. Her whole being centered now no longer in her external environment, in that room, but rather in the internal environment of her Eternal Self, of the Self which existed in the mind of God from the beginning of time.

If we had joined this family on this afternoon as a scientist, interested in the physiological changes occuring in its members, and if we had received the girl's permission to measure the changes in her body, we would now note that her brain waves had slowed from the normal, active rate of about thirteen cycles per second to about ten cycles per second. We would enter then in our log that she had entered the alpha state. We might also observe many other interesting scientific phenomena such as the fact that her breathing had become increasingly shallow. But we are not here as scientific enquirers. We are here as enquirers of a quite different sort. . . .

Now the girl's mind, before so quiet, so serene, becomes agitated and active once more. Into it flows the image of the boyfriend from the town she had just left. Again she lives the emotions and the stimuli of their parting embrace on her front porch two nights before. Gently, very gently, she returns to her mantra, again coordinating it with her breathing—"Jesus. . . mercy. . . Jesus. . . mercy." Once more she settles into that holy peace where there are no distractions. Where there is only stillness. And unity.

Some twenty minutes have passed since the music was first turned off. (As we shall see later, chronological time is of very little importance here.) Very slowly, gently, the father begins to repeat aloud the words of the Lord's Prayer. One by one, each joining at a different phrase, the other members of the family mentally return to the external environment of the room.

Just as each member of the family had chosen a slightly different sitting position and a personal mantra, so each person now concludes his meditation in a different manner. The father joins the palms of his hands together and slowly bows from the waist. The son straightens his legs out in front of himself and slowly bends forward, touching his toes. The mother, very deliberately, makes the sign of the cross. One by one, they stand up and they leave the room.

But they leave it a far different place than it was when they entered. It has become a holy place. What they have done there (note that family meditation was their very first corporate act in their new home just as it was the last in their old home) has somehow sanctified that space.

They will, with few exceptions, begin and end every day by repeating this act. Because of this, they will discover that the tranquility and the peace (yes, that's what the priest means when he speaks of "the peace which passes all understanding") that each has experienced during meditation will flow over into and permeate their entire day, the whole of their lives.

The door to the room is closed now. The walls allowed to absorb the scent of the still-burning stick as well as the scent of what has taken place there.

While the family remains in the house the room will be used for nothing but meditation.

Save perhaps, on occasion, for making love.

What is this thing called mantra? The word is from the Sanskrit and it means "to free from thought" (man=to think/tra=to liberate). Generally it is used to denote a single word or a short phrase repeated mentally in order to quiet the mind and thus to provide an inner atmosphere conducive to contemplative prayer.

But this is a textbook definition. It tells us what the word *means* but it doesn't tell us what a mantra *is.*

Let's do a little review.

First, let's remember that our true nature, who we really are, is not to be found in workshops, nor in the latest series of tapes by our favorite spiritual teacher, nor in the newest book about prayer (not even, sad to say, in this book). Least of all can our true nature be found by *thinking* about ourselves, by reflection. (Of all the people in the world whom I might encounter there is only one that I will never see clearly—myself. When I look in a mirror, everything I see is backward.)

Our true nature can be discovered in but one way. That way is through experience, through being.

Moreover, perhaps the two deadliest and most self-defeating games I can play with myself are to cling doggedly to my ideas and convictions of who I am and, worse still, of who God is. (Remember, he is far more than, far beyond, anything we can conceptualize or contain.)

Sadly, since I think that I do know myself and that I do know God, my prayer—the very gift which he has given me to enable me to know him and myself—becomes instead a way of reinforcing and clinging to my misformed ideas and biases about him.

52

I go to prayer with my grocery list. Instead of being still and listening to Him as becomes one who would learn, one who seeks to know, I go with the same attitude I take with me to a vending machine—"Lord, I want 'X'; I need 'Y'; and while you're about it, give my wife 'Z'."

Let it be said again then. The reality of my life is God's love. Period. This is the ground of my being. This is my center, my core. It is out of this center and from this core that I am. Apart from this ground I am not.

Given this understanding, prayer can be seen for what it is: man's yielding to divine love in order that the Father might have his way with him. That "way" is union.

End of review.

Mantra is the breath of life. Mantra is being mindful of that *which* we cannot live without and coordinating it with the One *whom* we cannot live without. Mantra is the mystery that begins as soon as we stop thinking and simply open ourselves to receive.

To say mantra is to become the lover ecstatically calling out the name of the beloved during intercourse. It calls forth, it creates, the possibility for even greater love. And—to push the analogy further—at that moment nothing else in the world matters. Least of all thinking. At that moment there is no desire, no need, to reflect on such philosophical and academic questions as, "Why am I here; what is the meaning of man; of God?" At that moment you know why you are here. You are here *for* that moment. You are here so that you might abandon yourself to the Other (who is not other) and to that love and be consumed by it and drown in it. And nothing else is...*nothing* else.

Recall the family scene in the bedroom/meditation room. The members of our family each began their time of sitting by saying a mantra. Then, as their minds quieted, they allowed even the singlepointedness of that mantra to slip away and each entered into silence. What was that sequence of events all about?

The most active part of you is your mind. If you have ever experimented with meditation you know that already. If you have ever lain awake at night, trying to go to sleep you know that. (Incidentally, there is a helpful analogy here. In "trying" to go to sleep we become even more awake. It is only when we abandon our efforts to sleep that sleep comes. So too with meditation. In "trying" to meditate, in "trying" to be contemplatives, we become self-conscious. Only when we quit trying, only in self-abandonment, do we permit God to have his way with us.)

The best image I have ever been given for the busy-ness of the mind is that it is like a tree full of a thousand monkeys, all simultaneously flying from branch to branch, chattering and screaming for attention.

Only one of those thousand monkeys speaks of God, only one is that single-pointedness in love rising up from the depths of your life, calling you to itself.

It is the mantra which stills the nine-hundred and ninety-nine and leads to the One we seek. Understood in this way, the mantra is not preparation for prayer, it *is* prayer, for in saying mantra we give ourselves up to the absolute love of our Abba, our Father.

Let me stop here and give us both a rest. Let's both listen to one far wiser than I who wrote about all this many years ago.

Another man might tell you to withdraw all your faculties and senses within yourself and there worship God. This is well said and true besides, and no sensible person would deny it. Yet for fear you may be deceived and interpret what I say literally, I do not choose to express the interior life in this way. Rather I will speak in paradoxes. Do *not* try to withdraw into yourself, for to put it simply, I do not want you to be anywhere; no, not outside, above, behind, or beside yourself.

But to this you say: "Where then shall I be? By your reckoning I am to be nowhere!" Exactly. In fact, you have expressed it rather well, for I would indeed have you be nowhere. Why? Because nowhere, physically, is everywhere spiritually. Understand this clearly: your spiritual work is not located in any particular place. But when your mind consciously focuses on anything, you are there in that place spiritually, as certainly as your body is located in a definite place right now. Your senses and faculties will be frustrated for lack of something to dwell on and they will chide you for doing nothing. But never mind. Go on with this nothing, moved only by your love for God. Never give up but steadfastly persevere in this nothingness, consciously longing that you may always choose to possess God through love, who no one can possess through knowledge. For myself, I

54

prefer to be lost in this nowhere, wrestling with this blind nothingness, than to be like some great lord traveling everywhere and enjoying the world as if he owned it. Forget that kind of everywhere and the world's all. It pales in richness beside this blessed nothingness and nowhere. Don't worry if your faculties fail to grasp it. Actually, that is the way it should be, for this nothingness is so lofty that they cannot reach it. It cannot be explained, only experienced.

Yet to those who have newly encountered it, it will feel very dark and inscrutable indeed. But truly, they are blinded by the splendor of its spiritual light rather than by any ordinary darkness. Who do you suppose derides it as an emptiness? Our superficial self, of course. Certainly not our true self; no, our true, inner self appreciates it as a fullness beyond measure. For in this darkness we experience an intuitive understanding of everything material and spiritual without giving special attention to anything in particular.[1]

Isn't he delightful? He makes you feel at home with him right away. But do you hear what he's saying? What does that sound like, especially what he says about the light and darkness? Sure! It sounds just like the introduction to St. John's gospel.

Here's some more.

A naked intent toward God, the desire for Him alone, is enough.

If you want to gather all your desires into one single word that the mind can easily retain, choose a short word rather than a long one. A one-syllable word such as "God" or "love" is best. But choose one that is meaningful to you. Then fix it in your mind so that it will remain there come what may. This word will be your defense in conflict and in peace. Use it to beat upon the cloud of darkness above you and to subdue all distractions, consigning them to the cloud of forgetting beneath you. Should some thought go on annoying you demanding to know what you are doing, answer with this one word alone. If your mind begins to intellectualize over the meaning and connotations of this little word, remind yourself that its value lies in its simplicity. Do this and I assure you these thoughts will vanish. Why? Because you have refused to develop them by arguing.[2]

You see, as long as we simply return to the mantra when distractions surface in our meditation, we are not empowering them and they will die.

One more...

Why do you suppose that this little prayer of one syllable is powerful enough to pierce the heavens? Well, it is because it is the prayer of a man's whole being. A man who prays like this prays with all the height and depth and length and breadth of his spirit. His prayer is high, for he prays in the full power of his spirit; it is deep, for he has gathered all his understanding into this one little word; it is long, for if this feeling could endure he would go on crying out forever as he does now; it is wide, because with universal concern he desires for everyone what he desires for himself.

It is with this prayer that a person comes to understand with all the saints the length and breadth and height and depth of the eternal, gracious, almighty, and omniscient God, as St. Paul says. Not completely, of course, but partially and in that obscure manner characteristic of contemplative knowledge.... Little wonder, then, that when grace so transforms a person to this image and likeness of God, his creator, his prayer is so quickly heard by God.[3]

He says it all so well. Especially when he talks about the "obscure manner characteristic of contemplative knowledge." That's what we mean when we speak of "knowing" by "unknowing."

There are no boundaries to the depth of this prayer. Like Peter, walking toward his Lord on the surface of the water, we stop when we think. As long as our sight is fixed firmly on his face alone we go on. If we don't think of anything we do not stop.

If, in our sitting, we suddenly experience a thought, a distraction, we simply return very quietly to the mantra until it draws our minds once again back into the silence of God. Merton once suggested, with tongue in cheek no doubt, "Sit there and think of everything and anything. Eventually you have a distraction about prayer—then grab onto it."[4]

Mantra is like a beautiful, graceful bird, gliding across the blue of the sky. For long stretches of time he simply is, wings motionless,

56

at peace. Occasionally he will flap his wings, gain momentum, and then—once more—glide, be.

We fear this silence. The monkeys come back to life and our minds raise countless objections to such a prayer. Know this: the fear of silence will destroy us if we don't defeat it.

At the core of the problem is our pride. We know that to sit in silence is to renounce the ability to go to God on our own terms. We want techniques in prayer and forms to our prayer. A certain number of pages to be read and marked off by bookmarks. A prescribed number of psalms to be chanted. Some way in which we can know, tangibly, that we are "making progress," that we "have completed" this or that spiritual exercise. Some way that we can assure ourselves that we have "arrived." We covet a "jackpot spirituality" just as we covet the jackpot in every other area of our life. We want to be able to say about our prayer, "Hey! Look what I can do." But the contemplative is least likely to have consolations in his prayer. There are no experiences to which he can point. On those rare occasions when he speaks of his prayer at all it is not the meditation itself to which he draws attention but rather the God whom he encounters in the solitude of his sitting.

The silence of the mantra is not a technique. It is not a series of collects which can be gotten through. It is not ten Hail Marys and five Our Fathers. It is Heifetz' violin to Charlie Daniels' fiddle. It resonates within us and we become absorbed in it and there is no one left to count, no one left to keep score.

Ultimately we must all learn that we cannot do that which our pride demands of us, that the terms under which we go to God are his alone, that we come to him with nothing. Poor. Destitute. Impoverished. Like little children. Silent, imageless meditation— mantra—is the sacrament of our poverty.

To take God seriously is to meditate in silence, to risk encountering him.

The word of eternal life is spoken in silence. If we are to hear it we must ourselves become that silence. Our sitting becomes our renunciation of all we have and our reception of all that is.

The one who sits isn't going anywhere because there is nowhere to go. This *is* God's kingdom. Here and now. The depth of the sitter is the depth of God, his width the width of God, his height and breadth God's height and breadth. The one who sits has been divinized through love, his soul mystically transformed through this one little word.

What does such a practice have to say in regard to the mystic's contention that we are all one? Isn't all of this solitary sitting pretty selfish? I'm glad you asked that.

If we are indeed one in him—lost with Christ in God—if I bear within myself the Christ who dwells likewise and in the same manner in each of you, if there is no duality separating individuals but rather only a Person who abrogates all duality and in that abrogation, that transcending, creates instead a divine unity; then each time I sit in silent meditation I do so not as a solitary, intoxicated with the selfishness of my own aloneness with God, but rather as one who sits for the world; as one who takes into that meditation and into that silence every one of you; *all* of creation; all that is.

In the end, in the fullness of time, it is the Father who speaks the mantra. The mantra becomes his Logos. And the mantra he speaks, which he has always spoken, from before time and forever, is *you*. For you were and are and ever shall be his eternal word, uttered in his Christ who is his every breath.

In the end, in the fullness of time, when you say mantra you are not speaking at all. You are listening.

As God utters you.

What is mantra?

On a wall of my office there is a poster. I found it while on retreat at a Trappist monastery. The picture shows a wide expanse of desert sand. In one corner of the sand is a blade of green grass. The legend reads, "Go into the desert not to escape life but to find it." That's what mantra is.

It is a blade of green grass, growing out of the desert sand.

Footnotes

1. William Johnston, editor, *The Cloud of Unknowing*, New York, Image, 1973, pp. 135-137.
2. *ibid.*, p. 56.
3. *ibid.*, pp. 96-97.
4. Mr. James Finley, a resident of South Bend, Indiana, and a one-time novice under Merton, gave me this quote during a conversation in 1983. It may well appear in the Merton canon but I am unable to locate it.

i read the burial office with a friend today
simultaneously
though separated by miles
i was there
and no one was
alone

life is not ended it is changed
reads the pro-defunctis preface
why weep
i'm not going anywhere
where would i go
enquires the dying zen master
of his grieving disciples

pentecost i suppose
is better than most for reflecting
that seeming ascensions
and thus goings
are really only illusory
that
nothing given is really ever
taken away
in spite of how it
seems

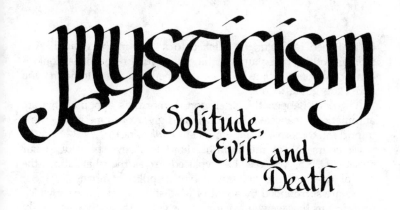

MYSTICISM
Solitude, Evil and Death

4

Wow! This is some party you have going here.... It looks like the whole city has come.... Champagne? Yes, thank you.... Is that caviar on that tray? Oh, I love those little Swedish meat-balls.... The band is great, where did you find them? Flew them in from Chicago, huh?... Just look at that gang around the pool.... I wonder what that funny white stuff is that those folks over in the corner are putting in their noses.... Dance? I'd love to....

...Would I like to do what? Well, no thank you. Thank you for the dance though.

Ahhh.... Could I have your attention, please. Would you all give me your attention? Up here, please. Just for a moment. Yes.... Yes, that's it.... Thank you.... Thank you.... Just for a minute.... Good.... I have an announcement to make.

You are all going to die.

And so, dear reader, are you. And so am I.
Glistening eyes today; empty sockets tomorrow. Our wagon

isn't hitched to a star, it's hitched to a hole in the ground. And there is nothing, absolutely nothing, that you or I or Johns Hopkins can do about it. Someday, one day, perhaps this afternoon, you and I are going to die.

If it does happen this afternoon, tomorrow's appointments are automatically canceled. (Which should give you some idea of how important tomorrow's appointments *really* are.)

Of course all of this is rather hard to hear, especially in our society. Death, you see, has replaced sex as the final taboo, the one of which we do not speak. Not in polite company.

We are surrounded by a glut of Madison Avenue imagery which promises us that we will live forever as young, attractive, upwardly mobile executives happily cavorting through an eternal cocktail party where the martini pitcher never runs dry and the supply of supple pool bunnies goes on forever.

And all the while, deep in our minds, there is a tiny—just audible—voice which whispers at the most inappropriate moments that it is all going to end someday. That we are going to lose the strength in our backhand. That we *will* eventually have to buy that first uplift bra. (Excuse me please, could I have another *Chivas* on the rocks? There's this damnable little voice I need to drown out.)

The thought of our own death makes our palms damp and the hairs on the back of our necks stand up. St. Francis of Assisi was wrong. Death is not our sister, but an apparition from another world, standing by our bed at night, drooling over us, waiting silently for just the right moment to stretch forth a slimy hand and touch our cheek with untrimmed fingernails. Death is a stranger, unwelcome, unbidden, yet always there.

We can't bear it.

So God bears it for us.

Suppose, just for a moment, that this was a lecture instead of a book and that I could make a statement of absolute certainty that at the end of the lecture, you were going to die, that that moment in time was, for you, *the* moment. Your turn. What would you do?

You wouldn't hear a word I said after that. You'd start squirming in your seat. You'd start watching the clock on the wall above my head (Don't move!) Every time I paused, your blood would turn to ice water. When I asked for questions you would have a dozen, a hundred. When I began to gather up my lecture notes you would leap out of your seat and scream, "NO, DON'T STOP YET!!"

We can't bear it. The knowledge of the moment of our death. So God bears it for us. He knows it but he doesn't tell us. Yet all the while he shakes his head in amazement at our inability to see.

For each of us has already died a thousand times.

Death, as the church has proclaimed for almost two-thousand years, does not end life, but only changes it. We hear this truth spoken at every funeral we attend and read it on every page of our holy literature and still fear own own death with an unspeakable terror that tells us another truth: *believing* (which is fundamentally an act of the will) is secondary to and often stands in stark contrast to *knowing* (which is truth "happening" to us and in us when we are prepared to allow it to be so).

As Thomas Merton once noted,

> When I think of my own death, if it fills me with an alien chill it shows me I have not yet come to terms with the resurrection.[1]

I may very well *believe* in the reality of the resurrection, my own as well as Christ's. I may be able to give chapter and verse on the matter. I may even go about mouthing comfortable words to the grieving. But until I *know*, that alien chill remains.

(The fact that as baptized Christians—or initiated Buddhists, Hindus, or any other religious people for that matter—we stand in community and confess aloud a creed while secretly repeating within a disclaimer such as, "at least I *hope* this is the way it is," fills us with guilt. Be at peace. The person standing next to you in the pew is going through the same litany. It's simply the contrast between believing and knowing. It is natural, and human, and all right.)

But the fact remains that, as I have already said, God has shown each of us time and time again that we need not fear death but only experience it as we experience everything else, by being simultaneously detached from the experience and totally present

63

to, absorbed in it. God has shown us by making death a part of life, by filling our lives with death. He has made it possible not only for us to believe but for us to know.

What then are some of these deaths: As with everything else I have written, you already know the answer.

In becoming adults we must first experience a death to our childhood.

Before one can enter college the high school student must die.

At the first sexual encounter the virgin dies.

The list is endless. There are for each of us of course more painful deaths.

I have experienced the grief and the agony of the death of a twenty-four-year-old marriage. (The fact that this relationship died sometime around its seventeenth year and that my former wife and I neglected to bury it until seven years later bears vivid testimony to how long we are willing to drag our corpses around behind ourselves.) Just as twenty-four years earlier on the day of my wedding I had died to being a bachelor and simultaneously been reborn as a husband, at the death of my marriage the single person was resurrected. The cycle of birth/death/rebirth continued when by God's grace the bachelor died once more in the fire of a love relationship which found its natural expression in remarriage.

Nor is death as an integral and normal part of life found only in the natural degrees of the cycle of that life and in our relationships with other souls. It is a constant also with regard to our symbols, tangible and intangible alike.

For fourteen years I lived out the warp and woof of my days totally committed to what in my more ideological moments I would have termed "the defense of my country" but what was in objective fact membership in the brotherhood of the merchants of war. When I awoke one night to the reality of my union with The One and with all others, the soldier died to that which was born in his place.

When one sunny morning on the streets of San Jose, Costa Rica, a small golden cross and its chain were snatched from around my neck, my identification with that piece of metal and its intrinsic meaning came to its end, its death, and was buried forever in my instinctive gesture of blessing the retreating back of the thief as he melted into the crowd.

Our guru is death. What he teaches us is that we gain all by losing all.

How does one come to this knowledge, to this way of seeing, to this which is so much a part of the mystic's reality?

The contemplative's understanding of death is born in the flash of insight that he need only stop the folly of thinking that he runs and controls his own life. In that fragment of time which is beyond all time, two things happen.

First, he stops worrying. He doesn't say to himself, "Now I am not going to worry any longer." He simply stops worrying. There is no longer anything left to worry about. And, of course, there naturally follows a rush of gratitude. He discovers that this gratitude is a way of being in the world, that it is *his* way, from now on, of being in the world.

Second, within there occurs an explosion of growth. Now growth does not come from guilt, or from anxiety, or from fear (I know, I've tried them all).

I'm going to digress here. The noisiest skeleton in the church's closet is named "Guilt, Anxiety, and Fear." It is uglier even than our shameful and sordid past of witch hunts and inquisitions and crusades. What sore on the Body of Christ could be more malignant than the perverted teaching that God's peace can be received only out of fear of Hell Fire, Brimstone, and Damnation?

My very favorite translation of the Bible, because of the accuracy of its rendering of the Hebrew and Greek texts into English, is *The Jerusalem Bible.* (Conversely, my least favorite, for the same reason, is *The King James Version.*) But there is no translation available in English that comes as close to capturing the meaning of Jesus' words to his terrified disciples in the leaky boat on the storm-tossed lake* as does the *New American Bible.* "Fear is useless," he says. "I Am."

The first time I quoted that in this present context to a group of students one woman broke down and sobbed uncontrollably. It was her moment of awakening. The next day she came into my office and without a word placed on my desk a framed piece of needlework which she had spent the entire night making. That is what her gift of love said—"Fear is useless. I Am."

End of digression.

*Matthew 8:23-27.

65

No, growth comes out of none of these—guilt, anxiety, fear— least of all fear. It comes out of fidelity to the love of God and from this alone, and this comes out of presence, solitude, and meditation.

> For us, solitude is not a matter of being something more than other men, except by accident; for those who cannot be alone cannot find their true being and they are always something less than themselves.[2]

True love requires contact with the truth, and the truth must be found in solitude. The ability to bear solitude, and to spend long stretches of time alone in quiet meditation, is one of the more elementary qualifications for those who aspire to have more than a nodding acquaintance with reality. How much solitude does the contemplative require? This much: Divine Union requires such a degree of solitude that you can't even take yourself along.

As a matter of fact, we can even go so far as to say that spiritual maturity is the willing acceptance of the responsibility for one's own solitude. Solitude is not some*thing* we are in; solitude is some*one* we are.

> A person is a person insofar as he has a secret and is a solitude of his own that cannot be communicated to anyone else.[3]

But there is another facet to solitude. Solitude and what it is we do by not doing within it—our silent, imageless, meditation; our sitting—is a kind of death, and at the same time, a preparation for the grace of our physical death.

Let me explain.

Meditation is not an action on the part of the one meditating. It is not something we "do" but a "turning loose," a "letting go." In the sense that something is being "done" it is being done *to*, or, better still, *within* the sitter.

We find this "not-doing" very difficult. It is hard for those of us who have grown up in a society where every value we have been taught is predicated on the need to accomplish and to earn, simply to sit and do nothing. Simply to be.

When we have been faithful to our practice for a while we find it easier to sit. What once seemed so hard now begins to hold some appeal. We begin to look with anticipation and pleasure to our times of meditation. There are fewer and fewer distractions. The monkeys become—for the most part—silent. No more do our legs ache, our noses itch. We have arrived.

Sorry. It's only the beginning.

Ahead lies an agony which makes the earlier *makyo** seem as a single raindrop in comparison to a hurricane. It is at this point that most of those who are going to abandon their practice do it.

What is this all about? What is happening?

Death is happening.

But be of good cheer. For it is not really you who are dying, but your masks. All the roles you identify with and take such delight in playing—these are dying.

The hard-nosed businessman—he is dying.

The benevolent father figure—dying.

The long-suffering mother figure—dying.

The straight-A, brilliant student....

The tweed-jacketed, pipe-smoking philosophy professor....

The "successful" young parish priest, next in line for a cardinal parish....

The vestryman....

The usher who forces himself proudly out of bed for the early Mass every Sunday morning....

All the roles that you identify yourself with, *all* dying.

What is a role? A role is anything in our life we have gained in chronological time and thus can be taken away from us in time. Taken as a body, as a group, my roles make up my External Self; my social self, my physical self, my psychological self...all of the externals. Those roles, that self, is going to die in solitude, in meditation. A role is what others think I am.

Frightening? You bet your life (no pun intended) it is. But wait. There is still more to come. Or rather, to go. To die.

In our meditation the False Self goes too. The self of my illusions, the self of my own making. The self which sees my

*Zen term for disturbing phenomena encountered in meditation.

own humanity as absolute. The self which sees my humanity as a way of gratifying my own needs. The churchgoing self which seeks to "do better" so that I can "get into heaven" to gratify *me.* The False Self is my ego. The False Self is the self *I* think I am.

This is what makes us fear the silence and the solitude. This, not the troublesome images we encounter in the early days of serious practice. To meditate is to come face-to-face with our own falsehood and this we hardly dare do. So we excuse ourselves by contending that contemplative prayer is not for us and we "say our prayers" instead, choosing the "Lie that is I" and clinging in fear to what we think of as "My Life."

Clinging to that which is not, and never realizing it. Clinging to what I am losing because of that very clinging. Every moment that ticks off the clock is a moment in which I am ceasing to be what I am and moving into what I am not. This is the clung-to life. And it is sorrow because I am clinging to something that simply is not there. So I never die, and because I never die, I do not live.

For those who persevere in the face of these deaths, there is a self that does not die. This self cannot die. This self is eternal. This self was not gained in time but before time. What remains is the True Self.

The True Self is the self the Father ever loves. It is the self which is the real you, the real me, hidden with Christ in God. This self enters the kingdom. It has but one act to perform—the giving and the receiving of divine love. It has but one name—the name known to God alone. It is the self whom God thinks I am. It is the only self that survives because it is the only self there ever was.

In the end, God will be All in All; only Christ will be in heaven. Loving Christ.

To enter into the realm of contemplation one must in a certain sense die; but this death is in fact the entrance into a higher life. It is a death for the sake of life, which leaves behind all that we can know or treasure as life, as thought, as experience, as job, as being.[4]

All through lunch the sky had become darker and darker.

I had been seated by the hostess at a table near the window overlooking the parking lot adjoining the restaurant. While I ate I had gradually become aware of the ominous stillness and—for lack of a better word—closeness, which those who live in certain parts of the country come to associate with the approach of a tornado.

Now, stirring a second cup of coffee, surrounded by the almost palpable wall of sound which exists in some public places—the clash of silverware, countless conversations competing to be heard-I became aware of a growing sense that I was present more as an observer than participant in the drama which was beginning.

As I sipped the coffee and lit a cigarette I could hear in the distance a siren cutting through the silence of the world outside. Still there had been no change inside. The conversations of office workers on lunch break and salesmen grateful for an excuse to leave their cars for a time continued unabated.

Across the street from the parking lot was a high-tech service station with neatly manicured lawns surrounding it. Spaced at fivefoot intervals on the lawn was a series of azalea bushes and it was to the changing configuration of those bushes that my attention was drawn. Ever so slowly—or so it seemed—the bushes rose from their beds and began levitating across the highway. Still, in the restaurant, nothing had changed. No one else had noticed.

As I continued to watch, the towering light standard in front of the service station began to bend at its base, lowering itself toward the street until it stretched fully across both lanes, now vacant of traffic.

There was one scream and the sound of a tray of water glasses being dropped to the floor and then the restaurant became a bedlam. People dove under tables, elbowing one another for the more strategic spaces of safety. The silence inside suddenly became one with that which was without. I saw a gaudily-painted van in the parking lot picked up and moved sideward, then gently lowered to the asphalt again, thirty feet from where it began.

An electric sign, still attached to its trailer, drifted through the air and on, past my line of vision, down the street.

I knew I was going to die. In that place. On that afternoon. I had been very close several times before and some indefinable but familiar presence was suddenly in that room, a presence which left no doubt about what was to come. Thoughts—these in slow motion— drifted across my mind: How will my wife learn of my death?. . . . I am glad/sorry she didn't join me this afternoon. . . . How will my children hear?

But—and this is what I want you to hear—that I was going to die *was perfectly all right.* There was no fear, and no regrets. Over anything. So I sat there and waited for it to happen.

The wind stopped and the light standard became vertical once more and the hush of the restaurant gave way to a crescendo of simultaneous conversations.

I got up, paid my check, and walked out into the sun.

Someone has written, "The realization of the *Self* can only be attained through the death of the *I*." Since so many Eastern spiritual masters have (probably unintentionally and unconsciously) grasped the true meaning of Christ's resurrection, much more so than have most Christian writers, this was probably written by a Hindu or a Sufi.

Of the meaning of such a saying we will have more to say in the next chapter, but my point here is, dearly beloved, that we have absolutely nothing to fear from our own deaths. Nothing whatsoever.

This is, of course, a teaching which is part and parcel of the catechism and the worship of the church; it is something all Christians have heard time and time again. Yet, as I have said, there is a considerable difference between "having heard," or even "believing," and "knowing."

Several years ago there was a death in my parish which was extremely painful to everybody. As I walked with the family and the parish through the early hours and days of their grief, I became aware of how much of the family's energy was being expended in attempting to choose just the right options allowed by *The Book of Common Prayer* for the funeral liturgy.

After that experience I devised a simple form to be completed by every person in the parish and placed in the church's files for retrieval at the time of death. The form tells what hymns and scripture readings are to be used, relieving the family of a burden at a time of trauma.

A marvelous idea, right? Wrong. Almost nobody filled one out. Not in that parish nor the one I serve now.

Do you know why? A lady told me why. To sit down and complete that form would make her think about her own death and she was afraid to do that!

How strange that we in the Christian world, who have been given the clearest possible teaching in our holy literature, that physical death is a divine giftedness which is but a passageway into the greater giftedness of fuller life, fear that moment in a way that is unknown to those of other faiths whose teaching is far less complete and definite.

My parishioner is going to die. And so is her priest and so are you. Moreover, none of us is likely to be particularly healthy when we die. The wisdom of the contemplative is that he is able to accept the anxiety of his own death and to realize the presence of God's love in it.

Several years ago I was called one afternoon to the home of an aged man who had experienced a series of strokes during the previous few months. When I arrived I found him lying on his bedroom floor, surrounded by the physician and the paramedics. IVs were attached to both arms; a heart monitor above his head showed jagged and irregular peaks and valleys.

I took his wife into the next room and we talked for a few moments and then prayed aloud. Then we walked back into the bedroom and she knelt beside her husband and told him that she loved him and then kissed his cheek.

I took her place on the floor beside him, whispered a few words into his ear, and made the sign of the cross on his forehead. That's all. When I straightened up the jagged peaks and valleys on the heart monitor had become a straight line.

Several days after the funeral the doctor called me and made an appointment to see me in my office. "I've never seen anything like that in my life," he marveled. "What did you say to him?"

What I said was something my friend had heard me say many times before both from the pulpit and in casual conversation. I had simply reminded him that it was all right to die and that both his wife and I would catch up to him later.

This time he didn't have to believe me. This time he knew.

The peace of the dying disarms us because it is the acceptance of the unacceptable; it is the denial of everything except love.

This is what happens when we sit in meditation.

One more story and then we'll stop.

During the T'ang dynasty there arose a ferocious warlord who determined to take by force all of the towns and villages in his region.

If the village had a monastery close by it was the monastery the warlord would plunder first, putting to death all of the monks as an example to the people of the village.

One day, as the warlord and his army approached a town, the mayor came to meet him on the road. "The monks have heard of your coming, oh mighty one," said the mayor, "and they have all fled in fear..." At this the warlord broke into peals of laughter and beat his breast in victory. "...except for one," said the mayor, completing his sentence.

In a great fury the warlord burst through the gate of the monastery and sure enough, sitting in the middle of the enclosure was a single monk in silent meditation.

"Don't you know who I am?" thundered the warlord, brandishing his sword. "I am Wu-ni, and I can kill you without blinking an eye!"

"Don't you know who *I* am?" responded the monk. "I am SuiTi. And I can *allow* you to kill me without blinking an eye."

What happens to the flame when a candle is blown out? It returns from whence it came. To its origin; to its beginnings. It returns to the eternal solitude of the unseen, the unknown, yet the ultimate reality which is the essence, the ground of all reality. So it is for us: when we are "blown out" we become what we always were: solitaries who are one with the eternal solitude of the All Holy; solitaries who are lost in the solitude of God.

Footnotes

1. *op. cit.*, Finley.
2. Thomas Merton, *The Sign of Jonas*, New York, Harcourt, 1956, p. 262.
3. Merton, *No Man Is an Island*, New York, Doubleday, 1967, p. 183.
4. Merton, Tape #276A. The Thomas Merton Studies Center, Bellarmine College, Louisville, Kentucky.

MYSTICISM

Who Am I
Who Is Not Who Is?

And now dawns the night
the time of darkness
engulfing
the flame
extinguishing
itself in itself by
itself.

Now
this very instant
the dust rises from the sea
the iceflow makes love to
the desert.

In the chaos of orderliness
is born that which
always was
to the delight of
One who always
is.

All that is known
(to be forgotten)
vanishing
in the dark hue of the night.

All that was given
(to be refused and in its
refusal embraced)
sinks into the deep
of no-thing-ness

For now our place in no-time
is sealed in the history of all-time
Now "we" are recalled
to space and place
and, refusing that,
assumed
into the zen-void
which is not
because it always
simply
was.

"We" who never were
have always been
"we" who filled each other's
thoughts, dreams,
days, nights, hours
bodies

"We" who are not
become
"we" who were not
and
in our naughting
at long last
are.

What indeed
happens to the flame
when the candle is
extinguished?

Does it cease to be
or rather
simply
cease to be
seen.

And likewise in our
own
darkness
do we
cease to be...

...or is it not
rather that
like all that truly is
do we not simply
cease to be
seen
while remaining
always us

Hidden
as it were
from all eyes
save our own
and
His?

5

The summer of 1982 was, by any criterion, the most tumultuous period of my life. As the balm of spring surrendered itself to the inevitable torrid heat of late-June in Alabama, I realized that almost every facet of my life—my marriage, my parish, my interpersonal relationships—*everything* had come unglued. Had reached the crisis stage. Critical mass.

I had a recurring dream during this period. In my dream I found myself in a raging ocean, tossed and buffeted by huge waves until, bruised and battered, I cried aloud for an end to the pain. Then I would find myself being sucked down into a vortex of that ocean. There the dream would end. I would awaken drenched in sweat and trembling. (The first time I had the dream and awoke to find myself covered with perspiration I thought I really *had* drowned.)

That I could not meditate during the early weeks of that summer filled me with an even more unspeakable panic, for always in the past regardless of the darkness of the night I had somehow been able to locate my center and draw from its core the certainty which would enable me to go on into and through the crisis of the moment.

Now it was gone, deteriorated into nothing. For whatever period I might force myself to sit, the act echoed in my present emptiness. Even my mantra, dimly heard in my heart/mind, was said as if by another's voice, mocking my attempts to relocate the peace of God within.

One Sunday morning during this period I spoke during my homily of the reality of periods of desolation in the spiritual life. I remember drawing on the biblical imagery of Christ's forty days in the desert as well as from St. John of the Cross and the concluding remarks of the conference Thomas Merton gave in Bangkok on the morning of his death, regarding the absolute need to abandon dependence on structures and institutions and to "travel light." I was, of course, speaking to myself as much as I was to any person in the congregation. (Most sermons—most good ones—have just that genesis.) I was preaching and the next thing I knew I was sitting in my office, at my desk, sipping a cup of coffee and listening to a tape of Gregorian Chant. Everything in between:

the Canon of the Mass, greeting the parish at the door following the liturgy, my church school class—all of it—was lost completely to my conscious mind.

I made an appointment with my bishop whose sage and pastoral advice amounted to "Work it all out but keep me informed; I don't like surprises."

My spiritual director listened intently, taking an occasional note here and there. When I had finished she sighed and asked if I had any explanation for the sudden appearance of a blue-green light in the mind's eye while in deep meditation. When I told her that I wasn't seeing a blue-green light in meditation she responded, "No, but I am and I was hoping you could help."

And so, one rainy but still hot July morning, I packed my car, said goodbye to my family, and began driving north. I came to ground, two days later, on the campus of the University of Notre Dame, at South Bend, Indiana. I had previously made arrangements to spend three weeks there to attend a couple of courses. And to try to be still in a new environment, away from my responsibilities to the parish. And to wait. For what I wasn't sure.

Those three weeks proved to be the most pivotal of my life.

The Roman Liturgy does not provide, as does my own Anglican, for a general confession at the Mass. For better or for worse, Thomas Cranmer's prayer book of 1549, the first manual for corporate worship for the Church of England, provided an effective alternative to the practice of private, auricular confession to a priest prior to the reception of the sacrament of the altar. I mention this because it is significant for what follows.

On my first day at Notre Dame I wandered, together with some eight-hundred other souls, into an auditorium where the dean of the graduate school was about to celebrate the Liturgy. I was more than a little familiar with the Roman rite and had no trouble staying with him—even without a missal—through the opening acclamation and the collects. But then the celebrant said a very strange thing. He said that it might be a good idea if we took the next few minutes to examine our consciences and then follow him in, of all things, a general confession. (He said this, *of course*, for me.) And so there was silence in that auditorium. While the internal litanies began.

In any other place at any other time the examination of conscience would have looked at the things I had done that I ought not to have done and of the things that I had left undone that I ought to have done. I had been through this many times.

But not that day. On that Monday morning, at that altar, only one conviction, only one self-accusation, would come. Try as I might— and I did try—I could conjure up nothing else to confess. So I didn't. Finally, I gave silent consent to what bubbled beneath the surface and I gave voice to my confession:

"Forgive me, Father, for not being who I am."

As it would several more times during those twenty-one days, the ceiling blew away.

For the contemplative, there is no cogito ("I think") and no ergo ("therefore") but only SUM, I am. Not in the sense of futile assertion of our individuality as ultimately real, but in the humble realization of our mysterious being as persons in whom God dwells, with infinite sweetness and inalienable power.[1]

Who am I, who is not, who is?

Well, for starter, *who* is asking the question?

It is an ego question. It was my identification with my ego that had brought me to the point of near-madness that summer. It is identification with our egos that makes that question seem so important.

We do not experience ourselves as we are. To the extent that I have identified my life with my thoughts of myself or with my achievements, the touch of God is death to me. That was what was happening. I was dying.

I was dying because I was simultaneously courting ecclesiastical success (with profound emphasis on the noun) and at the same time consciously providing in my life spaces of silence in which I was making myself available to the touch of God.

(Another reason for my agony was the web of falsity that the person who was then my wife and I had spun for ourselves in our marriage and my fear of shredding that web. I'll say no more about this facet of my life save only that my experiences at South

Bend gave me new insights, courage and fresh resolve here as well.)

My book *The Mystic Journey* had been published in the winter of 1979 and there had followed from some corners of the church a certain measure of praise and acclaim. The letters that arrived following its publication were uniformly positive. I heard from seminary classmates. I heard from people I had never met and would never meet. I heard from people asking for spiritual direction by mail. All of that, I assure you, felt very good indeed.

If you read that book, you found that it is more than a little bit academic in tone, and that is what I began to think myself to be. An academic. An expert on the history of mysticism.

That creation of my own ego was what I began to identify with. All the while I was making time to sit, making time to be alone with God. The two could not coexist.

Something had to give because contemplation is living without the assurances the ego can provide, the conscious abandonment of the desire for "success" in the ecclesiastical arena just as in any other arena.

These truths the would-be contemplative (paradoxically, probably the best way to become a contemplative is to desire with all of your heart *not* to be one) must eventually come to terms with.

You know what I am going to tell you next. You've known it all along. Here it is: *It is the ego which must be put to death.* In each of us.

The ego is an illusion. The ego is the bastard creation of my own Genesis myth. The ego (like rush hour) has no ontology in the mind of God. The ego is false. The ego is not.

To all the psychologists out there, professional as well as amateur: You're right; that does in fact disallow the theory that each of us possesses something called an "individuality." Possessing an individual self is simply another way of talking about the False Self.

Dearly beloved, God did not create us to "possess" anything. He created us to participate in the love which is the Divine Trinity. When he created us, he created a bride for the Word.

Only that.

Nothing else.

Everything else we "create" ourselves on our own without God. That is not making love. That is masturbation.

Somewhere over in the far corner of the room I hear a question being raised...

"Hey, now, wait a minute. This is some pretty heady stuff you're handing out! I'll stay with you for a little bit longer but my logic demands some equal time. First of all, if the ego, as our own creation and apart from God, must die, what then is left? And second, what about the original question? I mean, 'bride for the Word' and 'created to participate in the love which is the Divine Trinity' all *sound* nice but what does that *mean?* In other words: *who am I?*"

Good questions. They are both ego questions, but I'll try to respond to them nonetheless.

First let me tell two other things that happened to me that summer.

One morning, about two o'clock, I was awakened by a thunderstorm. I am one of those strange people who has always loved thunderstorms. Until you experience a thunderstorm in the flatlands of the Midwest, you don't really know what a thunderstorm is. I love the explosion of the thunder. (Recently my wife ruined an entire day for me by telling me that my life-long belief that thunder is caused by the clouds bumping into one another has no basis in fact.) I love the jagged swords of lightning racing across the sky. I love the sound and the sight of the rain demanding entrance to my shelter. That particular morning I got up from my bed in the dormitory, moved a chair over to the window, and sat there in the darkness simply being with the storm.

One of the reasons I feel as I do about thunderstorms is that they have always helped me put things in perspective. Their grandeur is so awesome that I had never, before that night, sat with one without coming away from the experience with a sense of my own finiteness and my infinitesimal place in creation. "Surely," I would think, "in the face of this awesome power and energy both I and my worries are small indeed." That night something very different happened. It has only happened one other time. I was suddenly and acutely aware that God broke through my reverie and said to me, "You are a part of this and this is a part of you. You are neither greater nor smaller than the storm. *You are he who is.*"

The other time came later that week. Late one afternoon I was walking across the campus when my eyes happened to fall on a large dogwood tree in front of the library. I was drawn to that tree, not in the sense that I had no choice, that I couldn't have kept on walking, but in the sense that it had grown on that spot solely in order that I might sit at its base on that afternoon. And learn from it.

So I did.

In fact I sat there for a long time. Holding up that tree. And it me. When I rose to leave I knew again what I had known when the storm had passed. I knew that the tree and I were one. I knew that I *was*.

I returned to my room. As I had done on the morning of the storm, I lit a stick of incense in thanksgiving.

With the death of the ego the "Not I," the False Self, is no more. Only the True Self, the God Self, the self which has existed—like the thunderstorm and dogwood—in the mind of God since before time and forever, remains.

With the death of the ego you are who you always have been.

With the death of the ego you are the one who is loved by God.

With the death of the ego you are the one who is lost with Christ in God.

With the death of the ego you come to know the secret of your identity; you come to know that this secret is hidden in the love and the mercy of the Godhead itself.

But with the death of the ego the question is not asked. It doesn't have to be asked. There is no ego left to ask it. It no longer matters. The question and the answer are one.

I don't, of course, expect you to accept these things simply because I have said them here. I know them to be true. Better yet, I know them to be The Truth. (The Truth is what remains when there are no experiences left.) But I did not know this until the time was right for me to know it. (This, incidentally, is what your priest means when he begins talking about *Kairos* and *chronos*. *Chronos* is linear or chronological time. *Kairos* can best be defined as God's Time and it has a way of breaking in on/to *chronos*.)

The questioner was right, it *is* pretty heady stuff. The best that I can expect is—going back to Gibran again—that what I have written might lead you to the threshold of your own knowing.

When you come to think of it, what do you need an ego for anyway? At worst it has an ugly way of becoming inflated and causing you no end of trouble with other inflated egos. At best it is simply a way in which we label one another and consequently avoid encountering, knowing another part of ourselves.

Let me illustrate.

Some time ago I was on a plane to Dallas for a conference. We were—like most transportation in this country—behind schedule. The plane was full. The stewardesses were harried and, hence, surly. The passengers, at least most of them, likewise.

As the miles fell away in the jetstream I could hear bits and pieces of conversations. I had closed my eyes, feigning sleep. (It's a good ploy in a public place, especially if you wear a clerical collar and want a bit of solitude instead of a stream of "Father, where is such-and-such in the Bible" questions.) I was amusing myself by eavesdropping on two businessmen seated in front of me. The older and more experienced of the two had begun the conversation by teaching his neophyte companion the ropes of cheating on his expense account. Now the subject had turned to the use of company credit cards for the procurement of prostitutes.

I had begun to weigh the pros and cons of "waking up" and ordering a martini, when a series of buzz words drifted back to me from one of the front seats. "Are you saved.... Your personal Lord and Savior.... Or you'll go to hell.... Burn forever.... Everlasting flames.... The Bible says..."

It had been interesting listening to the comparative talents of two professional ladies at an establishment in Reno by the wise-to-the-ways-of-the-world businessman, but I began tuning him out in favor of the unseen "holy man" up front. I opened my eyes, ordered my martini, and waited for more.

Eventually I saw the row where "the Lord's work" was being done. Just as I started on my second martini, a very attractive and very distraught young woman left that row and passed me on her way to the toilet. She was weeping.

When she returned, I reached up, touched her arm, and asked her if she would like to trade seats. "Oh thank you! Yes!"

And so the evangelist, a thin, disheveled man with tie and hair askew, found himself seated next to a parish priest with a martini in one hand and a cigarette in the other one.

He was, to his credit, taken aback for but a moment. "I see you are a catholic," he said. "Are you saved?"

I turned in my seat until I was facing him squarely. I looked deeply into his eyes, smiled my most pious smile, glanced briefly heavenward, and lowered my voice. He leaned forward to hear what I was about to say. "Sir," I whispered, "I am a Baptized, Anglicized, Byzantine, Buddhist."

The rest of the trip was spent in a contemplative silence.

The work of the ego is to provide us with labels. When the ego has died there is no further need for labels.

I could have answered him in a different manner. I could have spent the flight discussing holy scripture. I knew better. It would have been a very unpleasant afternoon for both of us.

Why? Let me give you a Cardinal Rule: Never Discuss Scripture With A TRUE BELIEVER. It will be the most fruitless, frustrating discussion you have ever had.

The TRUE BELIEVER has to be right. He has to be right because he is married to a book that has, for him, but one fixed set of responses to any set of circumstances, to any question. Life, he feels, is safer that way and he is no more likely to change his mind and test the freedom of his spiritual wings than that airplane is to turn into a cruise ship.

If you are attached to doctrines or to ideologies or to dogma to the degree that you have become an inflexible, walking, talking catechism machine, you cannot reach the highest attainment, at least not in this life.[2]

Our destiny is not to be good Catholics, or good Baptists or good Episcopalians or Hindus, Buddhists, Muslims, or anything else. Our destiny is *God*. Nothing less. That, dear reader, is The Point.

We have been given the freedom to attain that destiny. Total freedom. Complete freedom. Unbounded freedom.

Instead, we choose to remain prisoners to this or that creed, to this or that doctrine. ("Tell me what to believe and I'll do it.") We choose the bottle of Thunderbird rather than the Cabernet. We elect the illusory safety of our ego-generated labels to the God-intoxicated liberty to awaken and to be.

I know the anxiety all of this can generate, the fear, the uncertainty, the cold fingers of dread. I know because I have felt all that too. But know this in your anxiety: the number of hairs on your head is indeed known and the Knower knows what we need—we need him. He offers us liberation from concentration on the awareness of ourselves as separate and distinct entities, liberation to concentrate on the awareness of him as All-in-All.

"Follow no light save the one that burns in your heart," writes John of the Cross. "Send no more messengers...Gather no flowers..."

How do we do this? How do we say "yes" to the overtures of the Divine Lover to eschew all else and accept his invitation to the bridal chamber? How do we transcend creeds and boundaries and doctrines and dogmas and belief systems in order that we may become who we always have been; in order to become ourselves; in order that we—like the Beloved Disciple—might simply rest our heads on his breast? How does the ego die?

You know the answer already. I write this to remind you. By sitting, of course. By meditating in that interior stillness which has bid us enter into itself every moment since the day of our birth. By being attentive to the smell of the incense and to the sound of the silence.

For it is in the sitting and in the silence that all the masks we wear to impress the world and to protect ourselves drop away, and naked, without embellishment, we are finally real. Then, at last, we are true to the Christ, true to the Divinity, which is within us.

The manifestation of our True Self is always through Jesus, the Christ. This is so regardless of whether or not our individual cognitive belief system has incorporated him. This is so regardless of whether or not we profess to be Christians. The Christ, dear brothers and sisters, is universal. The Christ is the incarnation of the Holy Creator into the *whole* of his creation and you and I can be consciously as unresponsive to that fact as is the tree on my front lawn and it doesn't change the reality of the event one iota.

When Jesus says "I" and I say "I" it is the same "I" in the order of grace and love. Our True Self is manifested in every moment in which love catches us off guard just being ourselves.

This is how we sit. Unselfconsciously. Off guard. Just being ourselves.

All other forms of what we call prayer feed the ego, for in them we are *talking* to God; *we* have determined the agenda.

84

Only in that prayer which we call meditation do we come into his presence as listener. Silent. Open. Available. Naked. Still. Waiting expectantly on him. Making of our very selves a gift, the only gift we can bring to the One who is himself the Eternal Giver.

In our sitting he accepts the gift of ourself and—with great gentleness—strips it of all that is not us, all that is not our True Self. With great gentleness and patience he prunes and shapes us again into the person he first created us to be.

This process is all very much like the story of the Prodigal Son in the Bible. As a child in his father's house, the Prodigal had everything; his life was perfect. Yet he left that perfect place to seek adventure and gratification and success in a strange land, far from his true home.

We too have followed this well-worn path. We have left the Eden which is the perfect simplicity of the child: the paradise of knowing that what *is* is God's will and therefore that it is reality. The willingness to trust him and to let that which is, be. We have left the Father's house and sojourned in a foreign land; left God behind in order to go out and find him.

As we sit in silent, imageless meditation, we acknowledge our prodigal self and, like him, we return repentent to the silence and the simplicity of our childhood; we return to the Father's house. There, like the Prodigal, we are embraced by the Father's love. There we discover that our journey has been back into our original identity in God. In our sitting we have come home.

In our sitting there is no agenda, nothing to prove. There is but the perfect simplicity of being, of being in the silence, of being with the One who *is* the Silence.

Alone with The Alone, all of the barriers between who you think you are, who you would like to be, who your ego would like others to think you to be, and who you truly are, come down.

Who we *really* are is infinitely more than all our fantasies.

The final work of our meditation is the undoing of our egocentric ideas about the importance of our spiritual life and our ability to maintain it.

Our meditation teaches us that all of our pious planning—so many chapters of the Bible to be read each day, so many rosaries to be said, Masses attended, retreats made, daily offices chanted, Lents reading bone-dry "holy" books—all of it was self-serving, designed to earn what had already been given.

Our sitting gently guides us to a knowing which obviates any need for us to "do" or to "plan" or to "accomplish." And we have a *metanoia*, a conversion, from this to a willingness to abandon ourselves to an unmanageable love. Finally, we awaken to the discovery that our faithfulness to that love *is* our life of prayer because it is our very being.

This, I believe, is what Thomas Merton meant when he said,

> Prayer is our life; it is not sacred or secular...we belong to Him most completely in prayer because we are there most ourself.[3]

Let me offer you an image which may make all of this a bit clearer.

God stands at a celestial altar in some moment before the dawn of time. He stands there alone for there is nothing that is not God. There are no angels. No seraphim. There is nothing but God and that beautiful altar.

As he stands there, he asks himself a question, "Will you?" There is a moment's pause, like a hesitation. Indeed, it is a hesitation, for he knows full well what the cost, *to him*, will be. Then he answers the question. "I will," says God.

In a breath, there is someone there with him. That someone is us. God's "I will" is us. God "I wills" us.

Then he waits for our response; will we proclaim *our* vows? Every moment in the history of creation is *that* moment. Every moment is a vowed moment. Each instant of our existence is a vowed instant because he is forever vowing us.

All that does not come forth from this moment—all the anxiety, self-centeredness, self-consciousness, fear, everything that is not love—is not real.

Our awakening to this moment is our discovery of the kingdom of God because it is our awakening to the untold beauty of another from whence we have come and who loves us as we are.

And our awakening to this moment is one thing more. It is

our awakening to the realization that this is what is meant by the word "prayer."

One night during that summer at South Bend I had a dream. In my dream my son and daughter and I were busy with a tedious yet joyful job. We were pulling, strip by strip, long layers of dead skin from my face. It was like the unwrapping of a mummy. It went on for a long time.

On the morning that I left Notre Dame I packed my car and went back up to my empty room. I closed the door and kissed the four walls because it was there, for those three weeks, that I had been the most faithful to the vision which has been granted me.

The most faithful to the one who is underneath the layers of dead skin. The most faithful to who I am.

Footnotes

1. Thomas Merton, *New Seeds of Contemplation*, New York, New Directions, 1962, p. 9.
2. On this subject, compare Merton, *The Asian Journal of Thomas Merton*, New York, New Directions, 1973, p. 121.
3. Merton, Tape #254A, The Thomas Merton Studies Center, Bellarmine College, Louisville, Kentucky.

MYSTICISM
and Love

Speak to me
no more
of
pain and hurt and
greed

Speak to me
no more
of agony and strife and
hate

...Nor of
selfishness and
anger and
warring madness

Speak rather
to me
of newness and
beginnings and
becoming

...Of the
pregnant silence
of this
moment

Speak to me
of the
celebration of
life

Of the first
spoken
word of a
child

Of sycamores
born
from the
dearth of winter

Speak to me
of the soft
speech of a
brook

Of the binding
of
two made
one

Of bread
and wine
transfigured

into

The Word
made
flesh

Speak to
me of
you

And I shall
speak to
you of
me

And together
we
shall speak
of love.

6

Then Almitra said, Speak to us of Love.

*And he raised his head and looked upon the people,
and there fell a stillness upon them. And with a great voice
he said:*

When love beckons to you follow him.

Though his ways are hard and steep.

And when his wings enfold you yield to him,

*Though the sword hidden among his pinions may wound
you.*

And when he speaks to you believe him,

*Though his voice may shatter your dreams as the north
    wind lays waste the garden.*

For even as love crowns you so shall he crucify you.
    Even as he is for your growth so is he for your pruning.

*Even as he ascends to your height and caresses your
    tenderest branches that quiver in the sun,*

*So shall he descend to your roots and shake them in
    their clinging to the earth.*

Like sheaves of corn he gathers you unto himself.

He threshes you to make you naked.

He sifts you to free you from your husks.

He grinds you into whiteness.

He kneads you until you are pliant;

*And then he assigns you to his sacred fire, that you
    may become sacred bread for God's sacred feast.*

*All these things shall love do unto you that you may
    know the secrets of your heart, and in that
    knowledge become a fragment of Life's heart.*

But if in your fear you would seek only love's pleasure,

*Then it is better for you that you cover your nakedness
    and pass out of love's threshing floor,*

*Into the seasonless world where you will laugh, but not
    all your laughter, and weep, but not all your tears.*

Love gives naught but itself and takes naught but from itself.

*Love possesses not nor would it be possessed; For love is
    sufficient unto love.*

*When you love you should not say, God is in my heart,
    but rather, I am in the heart of God.*

And think not you can direct the course of love, for love,
    if it finds you worthy, directs your course.
Love has no desire but to fulfill itself.
But if you love and must needs have desires, let these be
    your desires:
To melt and be like a running brook that sings its melody
    to the night.
To know the pain of too much tenderness.
To be wounded by your own understanding of love;
And to bleed willingly and joyfully.
To wake at dawn with a winged heart and give thanks for
    another day of loving;
To rest at the noon hour and meditate love's ecstasy;
To return home at eventide with gratitude;
And then to sleep with a prayer for the beloved in your
    heart and a song of praise upon your lips.[1]

I am going to share with you now the Great Secret of this endeavor that we call life. I will tell you the answer to the question which every person in all generations spends his lifetime asking. I am about to place in your hands the Holy Grail, entrusting it forever into your care. When you have read what comes next you will have transcended the accumulated wisdom of the ages. You are about to become rich beyond measure, beyond your wildest dreams. The Pearl of Great Price is about to be yours.

Are you ready? You probably should sit down for this.

THE ONLY THING THAT TRULY IS IS LOVE.

That is all you really ever need to know.

St. Paul didn't go quite far enough; love is not the greatest thing, love is the *only* thing.

All of what we see going on about us and consequently think of as reality depends for existence on the one uncontingent reality which is love. All entities, circumstances, events, or acts not grounded in love have no basis in actual, ontological reality in the Mind of God and thus they simply are not.

But indeed we exist solely for this, to be the place He has chosen for His presence, His manifestation in the world, His epiphany . . . if we once began to recognize, humbly and truly, the real value of our own self, we would see that this value was the sign of God in our being, the signature of God upon our being. Fortunately, the love of our fellow man is given us as the way of realizing this. . . . It is the love of my lover, my brother or my child that sees God in me, makes God credible to myself in me. And it is my love for my lover, my child, my brother, that enables me to show God to him or her in himself or herself. Love is the epiphany of God in our poverty.[2]

Take a few minutes to digest that. Now you know why I suggested that you sit down.

Are you ready to go on? There's more.
Not only is love the only thing that is but

THERE IS ONLY ONE LOVE

That is the love of God for his created order, for everyone and everything he has made. His *unconditional* love for all that is. With no exceptions.

That means that I do not love my wife, or my children, or the people in my parish at all. Neither do you love even those persons in your own life for whom you feel a special attraction and with whom you share deep, intense intimacy.

The reality is far better than what you thought was reality. God graciously lavishes upon all of us the one love which is himself and—as if that weren't enough—he goes even further and invites us to jump into the very depths of it and literally wallow in the stuff ("measure upon measure, pressed down and running over") with him for all eternity. He shares it. He gives it away. It goes on forever.

As Merton puts it, typically poetically,

Love comes out of God and gathers us to God in order to pour itself back into God through all of us and bring us all back to Him on the tide of His own infinite mercy.

So we all become doors and windows through which God shines back into His own house.[3]

He says to Dick, "I love Jane endlessly and absolutely; why don't you enter into the mainstream of my love for her and I'll invite her to join me in my love for you."

The reason that that is better is because now Dick doesn't have to *do* anything. Dick never could do anything to make love happen. How could he? Love is a gift and as with any other gift all Dick (and you, and I, and all the rest of us) can "do" is to be open to it, prepare himself to receive it.

Knowing this, Dick no longer looks deeply and adoringly into Jane's eyes and whispers, "I love you." Instead, lost in the wonder of that which has been given, of that which is, each says to the other—when words are appropriate—"I am *in* love with you." But mostly they say nothing at all. Mostly they give silent thanks for the love they are in.

Of course this principle is not limited to the love relationship between two persons. It is a divine constant which holds true in every aspect of our lives, even that of our love for God himself. The fourteenth century German mystic, Meister Eckhart, said it best (and in the Christian tradition, perhaps first) when he noted that, "In giving us His love, God has given us the Holy Ghost so that we can love Him with the love wherewith He loves Himself."[4]

Do you begin to see now why meditation is so important, so central to our lives? In our silent and imageless sitting we are in fact opening ourselves to receive that Ultimate Reality which is the love of God which is God himself. Because we sit, speaking no words and ignoring all thoughts, and simply being, we learn in our prayer that love cannot be manipulated, or evaluated, or measured, but only received. We learn that intimacy with God never needs to be produced but needs only a chance to manifest itself. We learn that alone with God in naked faith, a simple love clings to no idea, turns to no created thing.

In the moment of that learning our meditation becomes much more than one more form of prayer. In the ecstasy of that moment it becomes for us a paradigm for the whole of our life.

Drawing us into his love, which is himself, is the nature of God, just as consenting to be drawn back into him, returning to our Source, is the nature of our True Self. This is the meaning of the term in Christian mystical literature, "mystical union."

Unfortunately, because we so often live in and from our numerous false selves, that union is delayed sometimes for a lifetime.

Because God has intended from the beginning that life should be an ongoing act of the reciprocation of divine love, a life lived in refusal of reciprocity is a life lived in torment. This is hell.

That so many of us live in that hell day after day, terrified to trust for even five minutes the silence in which God waits to be heard, is not entirely imputable to the individual person. The church must bear a large measure of the responsibility for humanity's torment and agony.

Early in its history the body politic of Christendom discovered that there were dividends to be paid to, and a distinct advantage for, its hierarchy if the church disallowed (or at least minimized) the possibility of direct and intimate interaction between God and man. Such a covenant of love at the individual and personal level could result in the loss of power and authority for the institutional body itself. What was promulgated by the early bishops and has been jealously guarded through the centuries, was a doctrine of mediated, not direct, grace. God loves and nurtures his children through the sacraments which are controlled and dispensed by the church. God reveals himself through holy scripture which is interpreted by the church. God does not interact directly with his children, but only through the duly constituted body. From time to time we have even gone so far as to proclaim the absurdity that there is no salvation outside the church. (If we must have a cliche, it would be closer to the truth to proclaim that there is no church outside salvation!)

Should you think I'm overstating the case, drop by your priest's office some day and mention that you have had a vision in which Jesus spoke to you directly. Observe his expression. Note how quickly he changes the subject. ("Nice day, isn't it?") In nine out of ten cases you will be taken about as seriously as you would be if you said your dog had begun speaking to you.

This has served through the centuries to keep ninety-nine per cent of Christendom's population, the laity, passively dependent on the clerical hierarchy. To be sure no one got the idea he could survive for long outside Religion, Incorporated, there was born the Doctrine of the Angry God.

The Doctrine of the Angry God is the biggest lie of all. Any lie, however, repeated enough times with sufficient conviction and apparent sincerity, convinces people to believe it.

For many of us, the functional image of God we carry from childhood is of the Angry God. A variant of that image goes something like this:

> We are standing at the edge of a cliff, overlooking a bottomless chasm. On the opposite side of the abyss, at the edge of another cliff, stands God. He is beckoning to us, telling us we must cross the abyss and reach him. The abyss is "the pit," hell. Hell is a place of dark smoke, sulphurous stenches, and flames which lust to burn (but not consume) us forever. There is no parole from hell. Once you're there, you're there. Spanning the abyss is a two-by-four and there is no way for us to reach God save by walking it. But there are two more problems. The first is that the two-by-four has been covered with a thick layer of grease (God has done this to make the game more interesting, to make salvation harder for us to attain.) The second is that just as we get halfway across, God picks up his end and begins to shake it violently.

If this is who God is, I don't want to be alone with him either. It is not.

God is not mad at you. God loves you and wants only to draw you back into himself. God *is* love. Love *is* God.

Nothing else is adequate as a basis for living. Success, position, prestige, power, money, thought...inadequate. Love alone is adequate. Love, you see, precedes life. You were loved by God before you were born and nothing you have done or can do will change that. His love for you is absolute and unconditional.

If you are living on anything else than love you are not at peace and cannot be at peace. A child living in a home without love is a child still waiting to be born. A child waiting to be born is carried to some extent within each of us. Birth begins as soon as we stop looking and start seeing, as soon as we stop talking and start listening, as soon as we stop running from God and start sitting with him.

Merton explains it this way:

> I who am without love cannot become love unless Love indentifies me with Himself. But if He sends His own Love, Himself, to act and love in me and in all that I do, then I shall be transformed, I shall discover who I am and shall possess my true identity by losing myself in Him.[5]

There is a point of no return in any love relationship. We reach that point the instant that we hear Jesus say "Follow me," and take the first step. To take that invitation seriously is to hear what those words mean: "Learn from me how not to run away from the advances of the Father's love."

> Occupy my whole life with the one thought and the one desire of love, that I may love not for the sake of merit, not for the sake of perfection, not for the sake of virtue, not for the sake of sanctity, but for the sake of You alone.[6]

So all of mysticism, the entirety of the contemplative life, is grounded in the love of God. Without that love there would be no prayer. Without that love there would be no "you" to read these words; there would be no "me" to write them. Without that love there would be nothing at all.

This love calls into being—creates, quickens, gives life to—all that is. This love binds together, each one to the other, and in the end binds us to the Source of that love, draws us back into the One whom we never really left, draws us back into God. In that returning we discover that there never existed a division between us and that—as we may have vaguely known all along— the whole of life is in truth one continuous mystical experience because it has always been suffused with God's love.

We discover that we have had from the beginning what we so desperately tried to create for ourselves. We discover that the drivenness, the obsessions, which marked our life had been phantoms—the bastard children of our own mind—born of the desire to find "peace at last." In our unwillingness to sit and listen, we had mistaken "peace" for "success." We discover that we had always been free to be.

We discover that all of the questions a person might ask about himself are irrelevant because they are questions about someone who isn't there, about a self apart from God.

We discover that every time we said, "I love you," those three words were spoken not to convey information but rather to evoke the possibility of the rediscovery of the ever-ancient, the ever-new—love itself. The words were said to create the possibility of more love.

We discover that Jesus came into this level of being to show us that we cannot contain the Father's love and that it is given to us in such lavish abundance so that we, like the Son, might pour it—"ourselves"—out; that we might empty ourselves on all that is about us in a kind of never ending *kenosis*.

We discover that we do not owe anyone, especially our children, anything but love. We discover that we do not have to motivate our progeny or change them or give them our values, that God takes care of all the rest through us if we simply love them.

We discover that the really significant persons in our life have been our spiritual directors, our soul friends (whether or not they were called that), because they helped us find the only thing we were never without—the love of God.

We discover that no stage of the spiritual life—life itself—is better than any other state, that the only thing that is better is more love.

We discover that many times when we wept for no apparent reason, without understanding why, our tears were a gift and that they had to do with our sudden awakening at the deepest level to the fact that in the midst of our own sinfulness we were loved unconditionally.

We discover that there had been nothing to learn because we had always known.

We discover that it had always, from the beginning, from *before* the beginning, been all right.

And finally we discover that it was all a gift.

Since I am writing these words on the sixteenth anniversary of his death, we'll close with a quote from Thomas Merton.

The most important thing in your life is something you do not understand and do not have to understand because God loves you.[7]

There are no words left.
The rest is silence.

Footnotes

1. Kahlil Gibran, *The Prophet*, New York, Knopf, 1970, pp. 12-15.
2. Thomas Merton, "As Man to Man," *Cistercian Studies, IV,* (1969), pp. 93-94.
3. Merton, *New Seeds of Contemplation*, New York, New Directions, 1962, p. 67.
4. C. deB. Evans, *Meister Eckhart*, London, Watkins, 1924, p. 147.
5. Merton, *ibid.*, p. 63.
6. *ibid.*, p. 45.
7. *op. cit.*, Finley.

Bibliography

Abhishiktananda (Fr. Henri LeSaux, OSB), *Prayer*, New Delhi, SPCK, 1967

——————-, *Saccidananda*, New Delhi, SPCK, 1974

Arseniev, Nicholas, *Mysticism and the Eastern Church*, Crestwood, St. Vladimir's Press, 1979

Brianchaninov, Ignatius, *On the Prayer of Jesus* ,London, Watkins, 1952

Doherty, Catherine, deHueck, *Poustinia*, Notre Dame, Ave Maria, 1974

Eckhart, Meister, *The Essential Sermons*, Ramsey, Paulist, 1982

Ferguson, John, editor, *Encyclopedia of Mysticism*, New York, Crossroad, 1982

Finley, James, *Merton's Palace of Nowhere*, Notre Dame, Ave Maria, 1978

Fleming, David A., editor, *The Fire and the Cloud*, Ramsey, Paulist, 1978

Franck, Frederick, translator, *Messenger of the Heart*, New York, Crossroad, 1982

French, R. M., translator, *The Way of a Pilgrim*, New York, Ballentine, 1974

Gibran, Kahlil, *The Prophet*, New York, Knopf, 1970

Groff, John W., *The Mystic Journey*, Cincinnati, Forward Movement, 1979

Hamilton-Merritt, Jane, *A Meditator's Diary*, New York, Simon & Schuster, 1977

Johnston, William, translator, *The Cloud of Unknowing*, New York, Doubleday, 1973

——————-, *The Still Point*, New York, Fordham, 1970

——————-, *Silent Music*, New York, Harper & Row, 1976

——————-, *The Inner Eye of Love*, San Francisco, Harper & Row, 1978

——————-, *The Mirror Mind*, New York, Harper & Row, 1981

Kadloubovsky, E. & Palmer, G. E. H., translators, *Writings From the Philokalia on the Prayer of the Heart*, London, Faber & Faber, 1951

——————-, *Early Fathers From the Philokalia*, London, Faber & Faber, 1954

————————-, *The Art of Prayer*, London, Faber & Faber, 1966

Kapleau, Philip, *The Wheel of Death*, New York, Harper & Row, 1971

————————-, *The Three Pillars of Zen*, Garden City, Doubleday, 1980

————————-, *Zen, Dawn in the West*, Garden City, Doubleday, 1980

Leech, Kenneth, *Soul Friend*, London, Sheldon, 1977

Main, John, *Word Into Silence*, New York, Paulist, 1980

—————, *Letters From the Heart*, New York, Crossroad, 1982

—————, *Christian Meditation*, Derby, Grail, 1978

—————, *Death: The Inner Journey*, Montreal, Benedictine Priory, 1983

McNamara, William, *The Human Adventure*, New York, Doubleday, 1976

Merton, Thomas, *No Man is an Island*, New York, Image, 1955

————————, *Thoughts in Solitude*, New York, Farrar, Straus, & Giroux, 1956

————————, *The New Man*, London, Burns & Oates, 1961

————————, *New Seeds of Contemplation*, New York, New Directions, 1962

————————, *Conjectures of a Guilty Bystander*, New York, Image, 1968

————————, *Mystics and Zen Masters*, New York, Dell, 1961

————————, *Zen and the Birds of Appetite*, New York, New Directions, 1968

————————, *The Asian Journal of Thomas Merton*, New York, New Directions, 1968

————————, *The Inner Experience* (circulated privately)

Nouwen, Henri, *The Way of the Heart*, New York, Seabury, 1981

Reinhold, H. A., editor, *The Soul Afire*, New York, Image, 1973

Ross, Maggie, *The Fire of Your Life*, Ramsey, Paulist, 1982

Russell, Norman, translator, *The Lives of the Desert Fathers*, London, Mowbray, 1981

Sjogren, Per-Olof, *The Jesus Prayer*, Philadelphia, Fortress, 1975

Suzuki, Daisetz T., *Mysticism: Christian and Buddhist* Westport, Greenwood Press, 1957

Suzuki, Shunryu, *Zen Mind, Beginner's Mind*, New York, Weatherhill, 1970

Theophane, *Tales of a Magic Monastery*, New York, Crossroad, 1981

Underhill, Evelyn, *Mysticism*, New York, Dutton, 1911

Ware, Kallistos, *The Power of the Name*, Oxford, SLG Press, 1977

Appendix

"After Silence, that which comes nearest to expressing the inexpressable is Music."

Some persons for whom silent meditation forms the center of prayer, find that a time spent in the company of a certain type of music is a time of preparation for their sitting.

It is very important that we understand that such time should be spent actually *listening* to the music, not using it as a background or "white sound" while we are engaged in some other activity.

The selections I have listed here are some that I have found most helpful in preparing for my own sitting. The reader may discover other music is more suited to his individual taste. Be free. Experiment. Enjoy.

SHAKUHACHI (Japanese Bamboo Flute) AND KOTO (Japanese Harp)
Zen, Spectrum Records and Tapes, LC 0846
Music for Zen Meditation, Polygram Records, Inc., V5G 8634
Heart of Bamboo, Hogaku Society Records, HS 204c
Oriental Sunrise, Plumeria Productions
Satori, Plumeria Productions, C-4302
Quiet Heart, Nimbus Music
Zen Waterfall, Global Pacific, 103

GREGORIAN CHANT
Grand Prix du Disque, Vol. I, Everest Records, 3346
Grand Prix du Disque, Vol. II, Everest Records, 3402
Grand Prix du Disque, Vol. III, Everest Records, 3426
Ave Maria, Phillips Productions, 7310 154
Gregorian Chant, London Records, 0S5-26431
Gregorian Chant, London Records, STS5-15578

CLASSICAL
The Four Seasons (Vivaldi), Allegro Records, ACS 8002
Symphony #6 (Tschaikovsky), Everest Records, 3115
Beethoven Sonatas, RCA, RK-1200
Albioni, Pachelbel, Bach, Handel, London Records, CS5 7102

SOUNDTRACKS AND GENERAL

December, George Winston, piano, Windham Hill Records and Tapes, CTC-1025

Chariots of Fire, Vangelis, Polygram Records, Inc., CT-1-6335

Jonathan Livingston Seagull, Neil Diamond, Columbia Records and Tapes, JST 32550

Gandhi, RCA, ABK1-4557

Introspection, Thijs van Leer, flutist, Columbia Records, KC 32346

Love Story, Paramount Records, PAS 6002